THE DOULTON STORY

PAUL ATTERBURY
& LOUISE IRVINE

A SOUVENIR BOOKLET
PRODUCED ORIGINALLY FOR THE
EXHIBITION HELD AT THE
VICTORIA AND ALBERT MUSEUM,
LONDON

30 MAY–12 AUGUST 1979

ACKNOWLEDGEMENTS

THE AUTHORS OF THIS BOOKLET WOULD LIKE TO THANK THE MANY ORGANISATIONS AND INDIVIDUALS WHO HAVE CONTRIBUTED SO MUCH TO IT, AND TO THE EXHIBITION AT THE VICTORIA AND ALBERT MUSEUM, *THE DOULTON STORY.*

THEY ARE PARTICULARLY INDEBTED TO THE STAFFS OF THE FOLLOWING MUSEUMS, PUBLIC BODIES AND INSTITUTIONS: ABINGTON MUSEUM, NORTHAMPTON; GLASGOW MUSEUMS; HASTINGS MUSEUM AND ART GALLERY; IRONBRIDGE GORGE MUSEUMS TRUST; NOVA SCOTIA MUSEUM; SYDNEY TECHNOLOGICAL MUSEUM; ART WORKERS GUILD; BUCHANAN HOSPITAL, HASTINGS; CITY OF BIRMINGHAM PUBLIC LIBRARIES DEPT; CITY OF BRISTOL PLANNING DEPT; CITY OF LIVERPOOL PLANNING OFFICER; CITY OF PLYMOUTH PLANNING OFFICER; COURTAULD INSTITUTE OF ART; GREATER LONDON COUNCIL HISTORIC BUILDINGS DIVISION AND SURVEY OF LONDON; HOSPITAL FOR SICK CHILDREN, GREAT ORMOND STREET; KING EDWARD VII HOSPITAL, MIDHURST; LEEDS CITY COUNCIL PLANNING DEPT; LEICESTER CITY COUNCIL PLANNING DEPT; NATIONAL MONUMENTS RECORD; NORTHAMPTON BOROUGH COUNCIL PLANNING DEPT; PADDINGTON GREEN CHILDREN'S HOSPITAL; ROYAL VICTORIA INFIRMARY NEWCASTLE UPON-TYNE; ST. ANDREWS SCHOOL PANGBOURNE; ST. BEDE'S COLLEGE MANCHESTER; ST. PANCRAS HOUSING ASSOCIATION; SURREY COUNTY COUNCIL; ST, THOMAS' HOSPITAL LONDON; TORBAY BOROUGH COUNCIL ARCHITECTS DEPT; WELLINGTON HOSPITAL BOARD.

THEY ARE ALSO VERY GRATEFUL FOR THE HELP OFFERED BY THE FOLLOWING COMMERCIAL ORGANISATIONS: BLACKPOOL TOWER CO., CARTER CONTRACTING, JOHN DEWAR AND SONS, DOVE BROTHERS, GLASGOW HERALD, GREENE KING AND SONS, HARRODS, HEAL AND SON, LLOYDS BANK, PRUDENTIAL ASSURANCE, REFUGE ASSURANCE, RHEEMCO BRISTOL, SELFRIDGES, SOTHEBY PARKE BERNET AND CO,.

THEY OWE ESPECIAL THANKS TO THE MANY PRIVATE INDIVIDUALS WHO HAVE ALWAYS BEEN GENEROUS WITH THEIR TIME, THEIR PATIENCE AND THEIR KNOWLEDGE. THESE INCLUDE THE FOLLOWING: D. BATTIE, MRS S. BEATTIE, M. BINNEY, J. BRANDON-JONES, A. CRAWFORD, J. S. CURL, R. D. DAVIS, R. DENNIS, D. EHRHARD, D. EYLES, J. GREENACOMB, D. HAMILTON, A. HARRIMAN, J. JENKINS, E. JUDD, MISS F. LOVERING, MISS J. LUKINS, L. MARTIN, C. McWILLIAM, MRS B. MORRIS, S. NUNN, A. ROWAN, J. SHARRITT, MR AND MRS I. SMYTHE, MISS Y. STOKOE.

FINALLY THEY WOULD LIKE TO THANK DR ROY STRONG, DIRECTOR OF THE VICTORIA AND ALBERT MUSEUM AND HIS STAFF FOR THEIR INVALUABLE ASSISTANCE AND COOPERATION IN MOUNTING THE EXHIBITION, IN PARTICULAR, J. V. G. MALLET, KEEPER OF THE CERAMICS DEPARTMENT AND HIS STAFF MISS J. BLAIN, MISS C. SILLAVAN, MISS M. THUNDER, AND C. TRUMAN; DR J. ASHLEY-SMITH, KEEPER OF THE CONSERVATION DEPARTMENT AND HIS ASSISTANT MISS J. LARNEY; M. DARBY, EXHIBITIONS OFFICER AND HIS ASSISTANTS MISS G. CUTBILL AND G. HALL; AND ALSO D. COACHWORTH, MISS J. HAWKINS AND C. NEWTON

PUBLISHED BY ROYAL DOULTON TABLEWARE LIMITED
LONDON ROAD, STOKE ON TRENT, ENGLAND

© ROYAL DOULTON TABLEWARE LIMITED

DESIGNED BY TRICKETT & WEBB LIMITED,
AND PRINTED AND BOUND IN ENGLAND BY THE WESTERHAM PRESS LIMITED

ISBN 0 906262 02 X

PHOTOGRAPHS SUPPLIED BY OR COURTESY OF BRUTON PHOTOGRAPHY, JUNE BUCHAN, COURTAULD INSTITUTE OF ART, RICHARD DENNIS, GLASGOW UNIVERSITY LIBRARY, HAMILTON DISTRICT COUNCIL, LOUISE IRVINE, LLOYDS BANK (KENNETH FENSON), MUSEUM OF LONDON, NATIONAL MONUMENTS RECORD, PRUDENCE CUMING ASSOCIATES, SMITHSONIAN INSTITUTION (WASHINGTON DC), IAN SMYTHE, SOTHEBY'S BELGRAVIA, JOHN TUSTIN, VICTORIA AND ALBERT MUSEUM (CROWN COPYRIGHT), MOIRA WALTERS

ROYAL DOULTON LAMBETH

CONTENTS

PREFACE

This exhibition of ceramics produced by the still vigorous firm of Doulton exemplifies, like the recent shows of Minton and of Poole Pottery, the Victoria and Albert's continuing interest in marriages between good design and industry.

Doulton's 'Art Pottery' in salt-glazed stoneware produced at Lambeth has long been appreciated both for its intrinsic merits and for its influence on the development of the studio pottery movement. But the present exhibition is intended also to draw attention to the relatively neglected wares of the Nile Street factory at Burslem as well as to the achievements in drainage and sanitation that formed the economic basis for so much else. Furthermore, the exhibition should help draw attention to Doulton's architectural ceramics.

The planning and mounting of this exhibition has in itself been the result of a valuable cooperation between Royal Doulton and the V & A, and we are all indebted to their very significant financial involvement. For this we are particularly grateful to J P Medd, the Chairman of Doulton and Company, and to R J Bailey, the Managing Director of Royal Doulton Tableware Limited.

The collections of Messrs Doulton and of the Victoria and Albert naturally formed a starting point for the choice of exhibits, but a great debt of gratitude is due to private collectors both in the United Kingdom and the USA who have immeasurably enriched the exhibition by their loans, for as yet there is disappointingly little Doulton in most public collections.

An essential element of this exhibition has been the design and presentation by Trickett and Webb Limited. They have approached the subject in a very fresh way, coordinating all the aspects of design. The presentation of the exhibits has been greatly enriched by graphic backgrounds designed by Edward Ardizzone, Glyn Boyd Harte, Ian Beck and John Ireland.

As for the planning of the Exhibition, the selection of exhibits and the writing of the present publication, this onerous work has been carried out in consultation with the Museum's Department of Ceramics by Mr Paul Atterbury and Miss Louise Irvine. To these and to many others I offer my warmest thanks.

Roy Strong

ROY STRONG
Director
Victoria and Albert Museum

In 1815, John Doulton invested his life savings of £100 in a small riverside pottery in Lambeth, South London. This pottery, one of many in the area, produced a range of utilitarian salt-glazed stoneware. Aided by Doulton's three years' experience as a thrower at the Fulham Pottery, and his hard work, the pottery thrived and he became a partner.

By 1826 the Company was trading as Doulton & Watts, and was already becoming one of the more important potteries in the area.

A few years later, Doulton's son Henry joined the Company as an apprentice, putting aside his interests in the non-conformist church. Dedication and personal ambition drove Henry Doulton to acquire quickly a full knowledge of all aspects of the pottery trade, from preparing the clay to selling the wares and so he was soon able to play a leading role in the running of the pottery. Under his guidance it expanded rapidly, swallowing in the process some of its less efficient neighbours. Henry then began to turn his eyes in other directions. By the late 1830s, architectural terracotta and garden ornaments were added to the range, but more significant was Henry's interests in sanitation.

As an intelligent and ambitious Victorian entrepreneur, Henry was probably without equal. It did not take him long to appreciate the likely impact of the sanitary revolution that was about to hit London and the new industrial cities.

The Lambeth Pottery, as Doulton & Watts was now called, began therefore to turn its attention to the large-scale production of stoneware drainpipes, conduits and related wares. This development was well timed, and Doulton products were soon disappearing in vast quantities beneath the streets of London and other cities. That many of these sewer and water pipes are still in use today is a fitting tribute to the quality of the Doulton product.

The Lambeth Pottery, and the Doulton family, benefited greatly from

THE DOULTON STORY

Henry's foresight, and it is important to remember that upon the firm foundation of these vital but unromantic objects was built Doulton's future reputation. Without the drains there would have been no Lambeth Studio, no Doulton figures, character jugs, tableware; indeed, probably no Burslem factory and no Doulton story to tell. One of the direct results of Doulton's involvement in the sanitary revolution was that the name and reputation of Doulton was

PORTRAIT OF JOHN DOULTON PAINTED IN 1872

spread far and wide. International Exhibition displays increased this still further and the company inevitably began to attract attention outside the ceramic industry.

One area of particular relevance was among the newly-formed art schools which were issuing annually quantities of trained designers keen to gain industrial experience. After a lengthy battle, John Sparkes, the Principal of the Lambeth School of Art, was finally able to persuade an unwilling Henry Doulton to give employment to a few of his students on an experimental basis. Limited to standard clays, glazes and kilns, and buried away in a corner of the factory, the first students produced their rather tentative efforts during the late 1860s, with design and decoration based on well-established historical styles. These early studio wares were enthusiastically received at the Paris Exhibition of 1867 and International Exhibition in London 1871.

Henry Doulton, whose success was based on his flexibility and his ability to seize opportunities that offered themselves, immediately gave the Lambeth Studio his full support and encouraged it to develop in a dramatic way. By the 1880s this Studio was employing over 200 men and girls. Co-operation between art and industry on so great a scale had never been seen before in England and, indeed, has never occurred since. The contemporary press was very enthusiastic; for example, in June 1885 *The Architect* stated: 'One of the artistic developments of the times – little short, indeed of a revolution – is certainly the one which owes much to the enterprise of Messrs Doulton & Co.' Inevitably, the quality of the Studio products varied greatly, and some eminent critics had understandable reservations. On 4th June 1878 Sir Henry Cole, the Director of the South Kensington Museum, wrote in his diary: 'Drove to Lambeth and went to his (Doulton's) works. Very large. He seems struggling into a sort of untrained style, chiefly done by girls. Every piece passes through 3 or more hands who do what they like. No modelling except a little ornament. One turns and bends. Another scratches ornament, a third paints it according to fancy. There was one Man an untrained genius who could model.'

However, the real significance of the Studio was not in its products but in its effect on the ceramic industry as a whole. The Lambeth experience encouraged potters, great and small, throughout Britain, to start art departments, and so ultimately brought about the rapprochement between art and industry that Henry Cole and others had dreamt about in the 1840s and 1850s. This new philosophy did much to enhance the prestige of British ceramics abroad, helping Doulton and other great manufacturers of the period, Minton, Copeland, George Jones, etc., to achieve a position of world dominance, the long-term effects of which are the basis for the continued stability of the British ceramic industry today.

The Lambeth Studios flourished and encouraged Henry Doulton to cast his eyes and his ambitions further afield. Having already established factories making sanitary, industrial and architectural products in Paisley, Rowley Regis, Erith, Birmingham, St Helens and Paris, Henry turned his attention towards North Staffordshire, the traditional home of the English ceramic industry.

In 1877, against all the advice of colleagues, critics and rivals, he purchased a major shareholding in the old-established Nile Street Pottery of Pinder Bourne & Co. of Burslem, Stoke-on-Trent. This company, a major producer of earthenware tableware and ornaments, also shared the universal enthusiasm for art wares. Other features which recommended it to Doulton were its interests in insulators and other industrial products.

This direct assault upon the well-entrenched fortress of North Staffordshire was badly received by the Stoke pottery fraternity. They closed their

DOULTON AND WATTS INVOICE OF JANUARY 1847 SHOWING THE LAMBETH POTTERY

PHOTOGRAPH BY WILLIAM STRUDWICK SHOWING THE LAMBETH RIVERFRONT IN THE 1860s

HAS

DEATH

(IN A RAGE)

Been invited by the Commissioners of Common Sewers to take up his abode in Lambeth? or, from what other villanous cause proceeds the frightful Mortality by which we are surrounded?

In this Pest-House of the Metropolis, and disgrace to the Nation, the main thoroughfares are still without Common Sewers, although the Inhabitants have paid exorbitant Rates from time immemorial!!!

‟ O Heaven! that such companions thou'dst unfold,
" And put in every honest hand, a whip,
" To lash the rascals naked through the world."

Unless something be speedily done to allay the growing discontent of the people, retributive justice in her salutary vengeance will commence her operations with the Lamp-Iron and the Halter.

SALUS POPULI.

Lambeth, August, 1832.

J. W. PEEL, Printer, 9, New Cut, Lambeth.

A BILL CAMPAIGNING FOR IMPROVED SANITATION, 1832

DRAINPIPES AT THE ERITH FACTORY

TERRACOTTA PANEL BY
GEORGE TINWORTH ON THE FORMER
DOULTON HOUSE, SHOWING THE
DOULTON STUDIO

AN EXHIBITION DISPLAY OF PINDER
BOURNE PRODUCTS DURING THE 1870s

A VIEW OF THE BURSLEM STUDIO, c. 1910

THE ALBERT MEDAL PRESENTATION AS
DEPICTED IN THE *GRAPHIC*

HENRY DOULTON WITH THE PRINCE OF
WALES AFTER RECEIVING THE ALBERT
MEDAL OF THE SOCIETY OF ARTS, 1885

ranks against Henry Doulton, regarding him as a southern upstart; they also made the fundamental mistake of not taking him seriously, having decided that he would soon be fleeing back south with his tail between his legs. That Henry Doulton was made of sterner stuff was well-known outside the Potteries, and, although his venture was not initially successful he did not react as predicted. Instead of withdrawing he increased his attack and bought out Pinder Bourne completely. By 1882, even the locals had to accept that 'the Doulton invasion' had come to stay.

With Nile Street fully under his control Henry Doulton was able to consolidate his position. New ranges and techniques were introduced and skilled painters and modellers were brought in from other factories. The production of bone china was instigated by J C Bailey after another dramatic volte-face by Henry Doulton, who had at first totally opposed the idea.

At the Chicago International Exhibition of 1893 Doulton was able to show the world their wide-ranging production from both factories, when their display included over 1500 items, and received acclaim from the world's press.

In 1889 C J Noke joined the company, initially as a modeller but later as Art Director. From his fertile mind sprang the many ranges which helped to establish the Burslem factory as a world leader in both style, technology and scale of production. Decorative figures, first shown in 1893, were introduced as an ever-growing series. From about 1901 rack plates and Series Ware were introduced in a vast range of designs. From the experimental Rembrandt and Holbein wares was developed the popular Kingsware range. This led to the introduction of Character and Toby jugs in 1934.

However, Noke's greatest achievement was the creation of a range of experimental transmutation glazed wares that are at best as good as anything produced at Sèvres, Copenhagen, Dresden or even in the Far

East. These ranges, the Flambés, Titanian, Sung, Chinese Jade, Chang and Crystalline represent one of the greatest contributions to studio pottery made by a large British manufacturer in this century.

Apart from the many forms of tableware that supplied their bread and butter, Doulton also produced many examples of high-quality artist-decorated porcelain. These fine pieces by artists such as Curnock, Dewsberry or Allen were fitting rivals for anything their contemporaries at Worcester or Derby could make. In short, the policy of the Burslem factory appeared to be to produce more diversified products than any other factory, and to produce them better.

For these and other ceramic achievements Henry Doulton received many honours: In 1885 he was presented with the Albert Medal by the Royal Society of Arts and in 1887 he was knighted by Queen Victoria, the first English potter ever to receive this honour. When he died in 1897 he was lamented the length and breadth of the country. He left behind an empire that he had built out of virtually nothing. Under the direction of his lieutenants, his son Lewis, J C Bailey, John Slater, Noke and others, this empire continued to flourish and expand.

Diversification brought increasing interests in architectural, sanitary and industrial areas, particularly in the new electrical field. The Lambeth factory, still largely supported by sanitary production, was able to enter the 20th century with many new and stylish stoneware and earthenware products. Even the Studio was able to survive the transition into the post-war world, a period when the definition of studio pottery was being changed by potters who, turning their backs on industry, fled into the hinterlands of Britain in pursuit of some romantic primitive ideal. In fact, the Lambeth Studio continued to exist until the final closure of the Lambeth factory in 1956 and fought to the end for the belief that true studio potters could also exist in an industrial environment, the principle launched by John Sparkes in 1860s.

The final closure of Lambeth, provoked by rising transport costs and by the clean air legislation, was followed by a gradual reduction of manufacture in some other areas. Doulton concentrated their activities at

LAMBETH OFFICE OUTING, c. 1925

Burslem and in the sanitary and industrial fields. In any case, the significance of Lambeth had been slowly eclipsed by the developments in North Staffordshire which was now the centre of Doulton production. Henry Doulton's 'invasion' had succeeded beyond his wildest dreams.

By a series of mergers, first with other companies and then in 1968 with Allied English Potteries Group, a new major manufacturer emerged. Doulton & Co. today is the largest manufacturer of ceramic products in the UK, with interests in glass, industrial and sanitary wares, engineering and building materials. Royal Doulton Tableware Limited, the tableware and domestic products section, with its headquarters firmly in the Potteries, includes many companies whose names tell the history of English ceramics – Minton, Derby, Ridgway, Royal Albert, Paragon, Webb Corbett.

AUTHORS' NOTE: A number of ceramic terms have been employed in this booklet to describe Doulton products. These include Faience, Parian, Carraraware, Marquetrie, Persian Ware etc. and are used in the sense that Doulton used them, namely as trade terms. They are therefore not to be confused with the accepted historical meaning of the terms.

A VIEW OF NILE STREET FROM THE *POTTERY GAZETTE*, 1933

QUEEN MARY'S VISIT TO THE NILE STREET FACTORY IN 1913

The traditions of saltglazed stoneware manufacture, associated with the riverside potteries of the London region since the late 17th century, were not altered by the formation and growth of Doulton and Watts. In fact, for the first thirty years of its existence the Lambeth Pottery was content to follow the pattern laid down by its neighbours and rivals at Fulham, Vauxhall and in Lambeth itself. Products were mostly utilitarian, and were designed for cheap mass-production, with details and ornament kept to a minimum. However, among these jugs, bottles, flasks, barrels and mugs were pieces that hinted at future developments. The large Nelson jug and some of the spirit flasks, for example, reveal a command of modelling and detail that is surprising. Similar skills are obvious in the pagoda model which shows an interest in architectural

Lambeth Pottery.
DOULTON & WATTS,
— 15 —
HIGH STREET,
LAMBETH.

EARLY LAMBETH WARES

fantasy more in keeping with the 18th century than the 19th.

During this early period, the fac-

tory concentrated on survival. Financial stability was gradually achieved, based on a thorough understanding of the demands of the market, and on a complete confidence in the technology of saltglazed firing. The firm's finances became stronger with Henry Doulton's diversification into architectural terracotta and his involvement in the sanitary revolution. The time was now right for him to consider the artistic status of his products. Inspired by John Sparkes and encouraged by the early decorative experiments by W Christian Symons and other artists at the Lambeth Art School, Doulton finally realised that to produce and sell vast quantities of utilitarian and sanitary stonewares was not enough. In order to become a Master Potter, he had to turn the Lambeth Pottery into a centre for the industrial manufacture of decorative stoneware.

A RANGE OF HUNTING WARE ILLUSTRATED IN DOULTON'S CATALOGUE OF 1930. THIS TRADITIONAL DOULTON PRODUCT WAS FIRST MADE IN THE 1840s AND WAS STILL IN PRODUCTION VIRTUALLY UNCHANGED NINETY YEARS LATER

A LARGE, LIGHT BROWN STONEWARE FIGURE JUG OF LORD NELSON, DOULTON AND WATTS, c. 1830

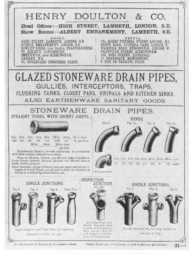

A CATALOGUE PAGE SHOWING DOULTON'S STONEWARE DRAIN PIPES. IT IS IMPORTANT TO REMEMBER THAT FUTURE DEVELOPMENTS AT ALL DOULTON FACTORIES WERE FOUNDED UPON THE SUCCESS OF THESE UTILITARIAN WARES

A DARK BROWN STONEWARE SPIRIT
FLASK IN THE FORM OF A PISTOL,
DOULTON AND WATTS, c. 1830. SPIRIT
FLASKS WERE MADE IN A VARIETY OF
UNUSUAL SHAPES,
INCLUDING BOOKS, CLOCKS, POWDER
FLASKS AND ALSO PORTRAITS
OF CELEBRITIES

A BROWN STONEWARE SPILL OR FLOWER
HOLDER IN THE FORM OF A HEDGEHOG,
DOULTON AND WATTS, c. 1840

A BROWN STONEWARE PAGODA
DECORATED WITH ELABORATE
FRETWORK AND IMPRESSED DECORATION,
c. 1860. THIS ORNAMENTAL PIECE
ANTICIPATES LATER ART POTTERY AND
SCULPTURE

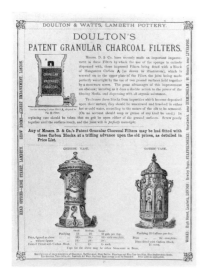

A DOULTON CATALOGUE PAGE SHOWING
EARLY STONEWARE FILTERS

A VASE IN CREAM-COLOURED
STONEWARE WITH SCRATCH BLUE
DECORATION,
NO ARTIST'S MARK, 1871. THIS SIMPLE,
DECORATIVE PIECE ILLUSTRATES THE
TRANSITION FROM UTILITARIAN WARES
TO THE ART PRODUCTIONS OF THE
STUDIO

Henry Doulton well understood the potential of national and international exhibitions as a means of promoting the Doulton name, and so he made it the policy for the company to display their products as widely as possible during the latter part of the 19th century. In the process Doulton achieved a world-wide reputation, and gained an outstanding number of medals and awards.

At first, at Hyde Park in 1851 and at other trade and public exhibitions in Britain, the displays were limited to industrial and sanitary products, which were, nevertheless, well received. However, at the Paris Exhibition of 1867, Doulton showed their first art wares. These experi-mental pieces were highly acclaimed, and so Henry Doulton was persuaded to enter a far more substantial and varied range of studio-designed wares in the South Kensington Exhibitions of 1871 and 1872. These displays were even more successful, with examples passing into the Royal Collections.

GREAT EXHIBITIONS

THE DOULTON PAVILION AT THE GLASGOW INTERNATIONAL EXHIBITION 1888. THIS INDIAN STYLE STRUCTURE, DESIGNED BY A E PEARCE, WAS BUILT OF GLAZED AND ENAMELLED TERRACOTTA WITH STAINED GLASS, ALSO MANUFACTURED BY DOULTONS, IN THE CLERESTORY. A VERY SIMILAR PAVILION HOUSED THE EXHIBITS AT THE MANCHESTER JUBILEE EXHIBITION 1887

By now convinced of the value of international exhibitions, Doulton seized the opportunity to show at the Philadelphia Centennial Exhibition of 1876. The Americans were greatly impressed by the range of wares, which included a number of vast pieces made specially for the exhibition. A succession of English displays followed, at Glasgow, Manchester, Worcester and elsewhere, but the zenith of Henry Doulton's career was represented by the Chicago Exhibition of 1893. This was to be the last that he supervised and it proved to be the most spectacular, with both Burslem and Lambeth artists surpassing themselves in the production of magnificent exhibition pieces, displayed in a suitably grandiose architectural setting. Many of these wares were also shown at Paris in 1900, but this display was enriched by many new pieces conceived in the new Art Nouveau style. This trend continued

at St Louis in 1904, but it was the launching of the new range of *flambé* wares that really enthralled critics and public alike at this show. These pieces were also the main attraction at Brussels in 1910, but the fire that devastated the exhibition also destroyed the best examples. The outbreak of war in 1914 interrupted this

A SELECTION OF EXHIBITION PIECES MADE AT THE BURSLEM FACTORY AND SHOWN AT THE PARIS EXHIBITION IN 1900. THE *DIANA* AND *LOVE* VASES WERE ALSO DISPLAYED AT CHICAGO IN 1893. THE ILLUSTRATION IS FROM A SPECIAL ISSUE OF THE
ART JOURNAL OF 1900.

succession of splendid displays, and only occasionally did later shows match the splendour and significance of the Victorian and Edwardian exhibitions. The Doulton stand at the British Empire Exhibition of 1924 concentrated on large-scale industrial, chemical and architectural ceramics, a trend that continued at Paris in 1925 and Monza in 1930. The new modernist tableware designs were also included in these displays.

In the 1930s, Doulton products of advanced design were often included in the exhibitions organised by the Council for Art and Industry.

After the Second World War, Doulton, along with many other potters, were able to relaunch their decorative ranges at the Festival of Britain in 1951. However, their greatest post-war success came at Brussels in 1958, when Doulton won the only gold medal awarded to a British pottery manufacturer.

THE DOULTON STAND AT THE PHILADELPHIA CENTENNIAL EXHIBITION 1876, SHOWING A RANGE OF LAMBETH STUDIO WARES

AN ILLUSTRATION OF TWO ASSISTANT STONEWARE ARTISTS AT WORK, TAKEN FROM *THE QUEEN*, OCTOBER 1887. THE LARGER OF THE TWO VASES, DESIGNED BY FRANK BUTLER, IS INCLUDED IN THE EXHIBITION

A PORCELAIN MERMAID CENTREPIECE,
MODELLED BY C J NOKE AND EXHIBITED
AT CHICAGO IN 1893

A TALL STONEWARE VASE IN MOTTLED
BLUE AND BROWN WITH A GREY LIZARD
MODELLED IN RELIEF BY
MARK MARSHALL 1904

THE *HISTORY OF ENGLAND* VASE
MODELLED BY GEORGE TINWORTH. THIS
LARGE SALT-GLAZE STONEWARE PIECE
WAS EXHIBITED AT THE WORLD'S
COLUMBIAN EXPOSITION, CHICAGO 1893.
ROUND THE NECK OF THE VASE, TWENTY
ENGLISH MONARCHS ARE DEPICTED,
WHILE ROUND THE BODY ARE TWENTY
ILLUSTRATIONS OF SIGNIFICANT
INCIDENTS IN ENGLISH HISTORY

A LARGE FAIENCE VASE PAINTED WITH A
VIEW OF ST PAUL'S CATHEDRAL BY
ESTHER LEWIS AND OTHER ARTISTS c. 1885

A LARGE PORCELAIN VASE PAINTED WITH
A CONTINUOUS PASTORAL SCENE BY
C B HOPKINS AND DISPLAYED AT THE
ST LOUIS EXHIBITION 1904

From its tentative beginnings in the 1860s, the Lambeth studio developed into the major art industry of the late Victorian period. Its story has been told many times, by Blacker, Eyles, Dennis and others, and by their efforts many of the artists and designers have become well known. Inevitably some artists have been unjustly eclipsed by others whose reputations have been based on the quantity rather than the quality of their works. The significance of the Doulton studios should not be assessed with reference only to the fame of its few first-rate artists, but also to the hundreds of others who were given an opportunity to develop skills within a secure industrial environment.

The artists were limited at first by the technology of saltglaze firing but gradually, due to experimentation by the art director W P Rix, the range of glazes and decorative processes increased. Rix was also responsible for the introduction of many new materials, first Faience, and then Marqueterie, Carrara, Silicon, all of which played a part in increasing the variety and quality of the studio output.

THE LAMBETH STUDIO

MARK MARSHALL WITH A EWER WHICH HE MODELLED FOR THE CHICAGO EXHIBITION, 1893

The decorative styles adopted by the artists were at first inspired by historical sources and were fairly pedantic. George Tinworth, Arthur Barlow, Frank Butler and others based their early work on 16th and 17th century German stonewares and various Renaissance designs. The incised decoration favoured by Hannah Barlow and Mary Mitchell was developed from the 18th century Staffordshire technique 'scratch blue'. With the increase in confidence and technical freedom came new ideas. The *pâte sur pâte* technique, whereby a slightly raised design was created by applying several layers of slip, became a popular decorating style with artists like Florence Barlow and Eliza Simmance. Contemporary design trends, including naturalism, Japanism and an interest in the arts of primitive cultures, were also reflected in later studio production. A feature of the Lambeth studio which is often overlooked is modelling. this was, in fact, the most original aspect of their production, as is made clear in the work of Mark Marshall, John Broad, Leslie Harradine and George Tinworth.

HANNAH BARLOW IN THE STUDIO, c. 1905

FRANK BUTLER AT WORK, c. 1905

A CABINET IN EBONISED AND GILT WOOD
DESIGNED BY CHARLES BEVAN FOR
GILLOW AND CO., AND INLAID WITH
STONEWARE PLAQUES DECORATED BY
HANNAH BARLOW. THIS PIECE WAS
EXHIBITED AT THE INTERNATIONAL
EXHIBITION, LONDON 1872

A PAGE FROM A HANNAH BARLOW
SKETCHBOOK, 1872

JOHN McLENNAN IN THE STUDIO, c. 1900

THREE STONEWARE TANKARDS
DECORATED IN DIFFERENT STYLES BY
DOULTON ARTISTS, LEFT, EDGAR WILSON,
1880, CENTRE, FLORENCE BARLOW, c. 1880,
AND RIGHT, MARY MITCHELL, 1878

A STONEWARE PUNCH BOWL WITH STAG
HEADS AS HANDLES AND A SILVER-
PLATED LID MOUNTED WITH A RECLINING
STAG, MODELLED BY GEORGE TABOR, 1881

A FAIENCE VASE PAINTED WITH POPPIES
IN BRIGHT COLOURS BY C VARGAS, 1884.
FAIENCE WAS THE NAME GIVEN TO AN
EARTHENWARE WHICH HAS BEEN HAND
PAINTED AT THE BISCUIT STAGE AND
THEN GLAZED. IT WAS PRODUCED AT
LAMBETH FROM 1873 UNTIL THE FIRST
WORLD WAR

A STONEWARE VASE WITH DECORATION
OF TREES AND RABBITS IN SHADES OF
GREEN AND BROWN BY MARK MARSHALL,
1903

A PALE BUFF STONEWARE VASE WITH
INCISED CHEVRON PATTERNS, PAINTED
TADPOLES AND RELIEF MODELLED
SEAWEED AND FISH BY HARRY BARNARD,
1882

A DISPLAY OF MARQUETERIE, 1892. THIS TECHNIQUE, SIMILAR TO 18th CENTURY AGATE WARE, INVOLVED COMPRESSING DIFFERENT COLOURED CLAYS AND THEN CUTTING AND ARRANGING THEM TO CREATE A MOSAIC-TYPE PATTERN. IT WAS DEVELOPED BY W P RIX IN 1886 AND MADE UNTIL c. 1906 WHEN IT WAS DISCONTINUED DUE TO HIGH PRODUCTION COSTS

A FIGURE OF THE ACTRESS DORIS KEENE MODELLED IN WHITE PORCELAIN BY JOHN BROAD, c. 1916

A GROUP OF DICKENS CHARACTERS MODELLED IN VARIOUS MATERIALS BY LESLIE HARRADINE, c. 1910

OIL LAMP IN THE FORM OF AN OWL, THE BODY OF WHITE, BUFF AND BLUE SILICON WARE, c. 1885. SILICON HAS A STONEWARE BODY, TINTED THROUGHOUT WITH COLOUR AND WITH MATT FINISH

A GILDED CARRARA VASE DECORATED WITH GREEN AND PINK FOLIAGE, AND SCENES OF CHILDREN BY ADA DENNIS, 1890. CARRARA WARE IS AN OFF-WHITE STONEWARE WITH A TRANSLUCENT CRYSTALLINE GLAZE, SIMILAR IN APPEARANCE TO CARRARA MARBLE. IT WAS MADE IN LIMITED QUANTITIES FROM 1887 UNTIL THE 1920s

A LARGE FAIENCE VASE DECORATED BY J H McLENNAN, c. 1890

When Sir Henry Cole, the Director of the South Kensington Museum, visited the Lambeth Studio in 1878, he commented privately that George Tinworth was 'an untrained genius'. He was not alone in this opinion, for both contemporary critics and later historians considered Tinworth the most original talent to emerge from Lambeth. Born in 1843, the son of a South London wheelwright, Tinworth rose to a position of eminence as a sculptor and modeller through his own endeavours. His education was rudimentary, he was largely illiterate, and yet he managed to make his way to the Royal Academy.

His success at Lambeth was in part based on his friendly relationship with Henry Doulton, who clearly saw Tinworth as a major discovery, and thus as a justification for the whole Lambeth Studio. However, Tin-

GEORGE TINWORTH

worth's fame was really based on his extraordinary versatility and his prodigious output. He was equally at home modelling comic mice and frog groups as major terracotta panels, and he was able to work at a staggering rate. His own religious leanings helped to turn him into a quite remarkable late Victorian sculptor, but because of his earthy sense of humour he was able to avoid the pitfalls that could have made his work pretentious and boring. Unfortunately few people are able to see beyond the religious subject matter and so fail to realise the strength of his fertile imagination, and his essential humour. Ironically this partly explains why his reputation today is not as great as it might have been. Tinworth the man dominated Tinworth the artist, and so he rarely receives his just status, not only as the most original Lambeth artist, but also as an early contributor to the development of primitive sculpture.

A STONEWARE FROG GROUP
ILLUSTRATING THE FABLE *THE OX AND THE FROG* 1881.
IT IS POSSIBLE THAT THIS PIECE WAS SPECIALLY MADE FOR HENRY LEWIS DOULTON, SIR HENRY'S ONLY SON, AS IT CARRIES HIS MONOGRAM

THE *MENAGERIE* CLOCKCASE IN COLOURED STONEWARE DECORATED WITH MICE, c. 1875. THE DESIGN WAS INSPIRED BY OBADIAH SHERRATT'S STAFFORDSHIRE GROUP, *POLITO'S MENAGERIE*

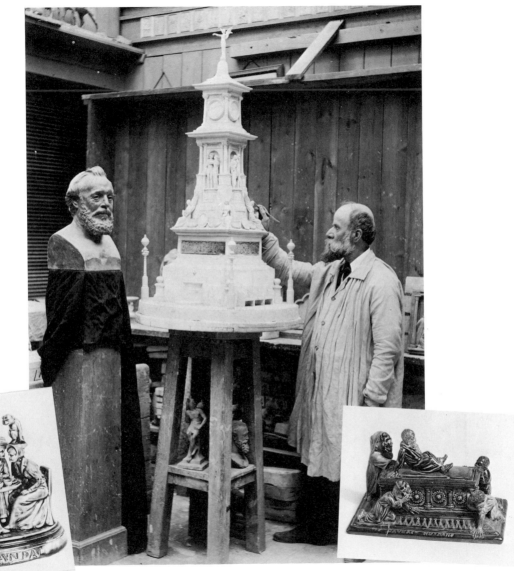

A GREEN GLAZED STONEWARE FIGURE
GROUP, *SCANDAL*, c. 1890

TINWORTH AT WORK ON A MAQUETTE OF
AN UNKNOWN MONUMENT, c. 1890. IN THE
FOREGROUND IS HIS BUST OF
HENRY DOULTON

THE DRUNKEN HUSBAND, A GROTESQUE
COFFIN GROUP MODELLED IN COLOURED
STONEWARE, 1881

The Doulton potteries were one of the major producers of commemorative wares over a long period. The tradition started with the early saltglazed face jugs and spirit flasks of the 1830s which commemorated a variety of political and military events. The celebrations that surrounded Queen Victoria's coronation and marriage prompted the manufacture of spirit flasks, jugs and mugs decorated with her image. From these early expressions of popular enthusiasm the Lambeth factory was able to develop a commemorative tradition that reflected all general interests, politics, religion, sport, war, travel, theatre and many others. Political and military events were the most widely covered. The South African War, the Trafalgar Centenary and the First World War were commemorated with a variety of Doulton products: jugs, mugs, figures, busts, flasks, tobacco jars and even teapots. Particularly interesting among the political subjects are the revival of figurative spirit flasks modelled to represent leading politicians in 1908 and also the satyrical

COMMEMORATIVE WARES

comment on the Suffragette movement in the form of a virago inkwell. A considerable quantity of commemorative items were produced to celebrate Victoria's jubilees and the subsequent coronations of 1902 and 1911, though it would appear that most Lambeth editions did not exceed 2,000. Probably the best known Doulton commemoratives are the

plaques made for the LCC and other bodies to mark places associated with famous people and events. A special department was maintained for the production of these until the closure of the Lambeth factory in 1956.

The development of the Burslem factory increased the range and diversity of subjects. From the 1890s commemorative mugs and other tableware poured from the kilns in quite surpising quantities. The beakers made to celebrate the coronations of 1902 and 1911 were produced in literally hundreds of thousands. However some are now quite rare, for example, the range made to commemorate the Australian Federation. The most distinctive Burslem commemoratives are the series of jugs and loving cups produced between the 1930s and the present day. These wares, with their elaborate and curiously crude designs modelled in relief and brightly coloured, were made in limited editions to celebrate a wide range of Royal events, centenaries and other occasions and personalities demanding popular commemoration.

A BROWN STONEWARE MUG COMMEMORATING THE CORONATION OF QUEEN VICTORIA WITH RELIEF PORTRAITS OF THE QUEEN AND THE DUCHESS OF KENT, AND ALSO THE ROYAL ARMS, LAMBETH, 1837

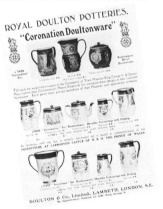

A DOULTON CATALOGUE PAGE ADVERTISING A RANGE OF LAMBETH STONEWARE COMMEMORATING THE CORONATION OF KING GEORGE V AND QUEEN MARY, AND THE INVESTITURE OF THE PRINCE OF WALES, 1911

A HUMOROUS 'SUFFRAGETTE' INKWELL MODELLED IN COLOURED STONEWARE BY LESLIE HARRADINE, LAMBETH, 1908

A RANGE OF BROWN STONEWARE SPIRIT
FLASKS DESIGNED BY
LESLIE HARRADINE, DEPICTING
LEADING POLITICIANS, LAMBETH,
1908–11. FROM LEFT TO RIGHT:
BALFOUR, HALDANE, BURNS,
ASQUITH, LLOYD GEORGE AND
CHAMBERLAIN

THE BURSLEM DECORATING SHOP AT
WORK ON THE COMMISSION FOR 100,000
EARTHENWARE MUGS WITH PRINTED
PORTRAITS OF
KING EDWARD VII AND QUEEN
ALEXANDRA TO COMMEMORATE
THEIR CORONATION, 1902

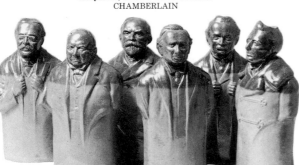

AN EARTHENWARE JUG WITH
BROWN-PRINTED PORTRAIT OF
LORD TENNYSON,
COMMEMORATING HIS DEATH,
BURSLEM, 1892

A BONE-CHINA BEAKER WITH GOLD
PRINTED DECORATION
COMMEMORATING THE
AUSTRALIAN FEDERATION,
DESIGNED BY JOHN SLATER AND JOHN
SHORTER, BURSLEM, 1901

TWO EARTHENWARE LOVING CUPS WITH
EMBOSSED DECORATION
PAINTED IN BRIGHT COLOURS,
DESIGNED BY C J NOKE TO
COMMEMORATE THE CORONATION OF
EDWARD VIII AND THE
CORONATION OF KING GEORGE VI AND
QUEEN ELIZABETH. THESE
WERE PRODUCED IN LIMITED
EDITIONS AT BURSLEM

TWO EXAMPLES FROM A WIDE
RANGE OF COMMEMORATIVE
STONEWARE PLAQUES MADE AT
LAMBETH FROM THE 1880s UNTIL 1956.
THEY WERE IN SEVERAL
DESIGNS AND COLOUR SCHEMES
BUT THE MOST FAMILIAR ARE THE BLUE
PLAQUES SPONSORED BY THE LCC TO
COMMEMORATE PLACES
ASSOCIATED WITH FAMOUS
PEOPLE AND EVENTS

When Charles J Noke was encouraged to leave Worcester and join the Burslem factory in 1889 he was able to instigate a revolution in both design and production attitudes. He became an Art Director in the broadest sense and so was able to affect all aspects of Burslem production. By his efforts a solid but unremarkable producer of earthenwares was transformed into the leading art manufacturer of the age. This was generally recognised at the Chicago Exhibition of 1893 where the Burslem factory mounted an extensive display which included a range of large, elaborately modelled vases finely painted by artists such as G White, and C Labarre from Sèvres, and a great diversity of ornamental vases and plates, with rich painting of birds, fishes, landscapes and cherubs, many with fine raised gilding, by a wide range of artists. It was clearly Noke's ambition to put Doulton on a par with Derby, Minton, Coalport and Worcester; in fact he attracted many artists from these factories, like

BURSLEM ART WARES

Edward Raby, John Plant, William Hodgkinson and Thomas Bott, all of whom helped him over the years to achieve if not exceed his ambition.

The styles in use at Burslem were as mixed as the wares themselves. Many of the ornamental porcelains were freely based on 18th century French

examples while the variety of naturalistic and landscape painting reflected an increasing awareness by the decorators of contemporary popular painting.

By his many contributions as a chemist and glaze technician, Noke also extended the range of Burslem products. He was responsible for the unusual Rembrandt and Holbein wares with their heavy, sombre qualities. He also introduced Luscian Ware, Lactolian Ware or enamelled pottery and the delicate Titanian range. These reflected an increasing dependence at Burslem upon the modern styles of Copenhagen, Sèvres and Berlin.

In the early 1890s Noke began to experiment with figure models. His first ivory-glazed figures of Shakesperean characters were shown at Chicago. From 1910 models were also commissioned from sculptors such as Phoebe Stabler, Stanley Thorogood, Charles Vyse and Albert Toft. From these beginnings developed the vast range of figures still in production.

C J NOKE IN HIS STUDIO, c. 1930

DAVID DEWSBERRY, AN ARTIST WHO SPECIALISED IN ORCHID PAINTING

PERCY CURNOCK, A FLOWER AND
LANDSCAPE PAINTER

A SELECTION OF PORCELAIN
PLATES WITH PAINTED
DECORATION AND RICH GILDING,
c. 1905–30. FROM LEFT TO RIGHT,
TOP ROW: J BIRKBECK AND
D DEWSBERRY; CENTRE:
P. CURNOCK; BOTTOM ROW:
G H EVANS AND J BIRKBECK

A SPANISH WARE VASE IN PURPLE AND
GOLD DECORATED WITH IRISES BY D
DEWSBERRY, 1884. THIS PIECE WAS
EXHIBITED AT THE HEALTH EXHIBITION
LONDON, 1884. SPANISH WARE, A POPULAR
STYLE
DEVELOPED BY JOHN SLATER IN THE
1880s, WAS A FORM OF RAISED GOLD
OUTLINE DECORATION

TWO EARLY FIGURES DESIGNED BY C J
NOKE IN THE 1890s DEPICTING THE
ACTORS HENRY IRVING AND ELLEN
TERRY IN THEIR COSTUMES FOR
SHAKESPEARE'S *HENRY VIII*. THESE
MODELS WERE SHOWN AT THE CHICAGO
EXHIBITION OF 1893

A TITANIAN FLASK WITH PAINTED
DECORATION OF A POLAR BEAR IN A
COPENHAGEN STYLE BY H ALLEN, c. 1920.
TITANIAN WAS A GLAZE
EFFECT INTRODUCED IN 1916 BY
C J NOKE. THE MOTTLED LUSTROUS
GROUNDS WERE OFTEN PAINTED IN A
DELICATE MANNER BY H ALLEN, H
TITTENSOR, H NIXON AND OTHER ARTISTS

A VASE IN LUSCIAN WARE WITH PAINTED
DECORATION OF A
CAVALIER BY W NUNN, c. 1910.
LUSCIAN WARE WAS A FORM OF
ON-GLAZE ENAMEL DECORATION
PRODUCED BETWEEN c. 1896 AND 1914

A VASE DECORATED IN THE *BARBOTINE* TECHNIQUE WITH STYLISED FOLIATE MOTIFS IN BRIGHT GREENS AND BLUES, c. 1910. THIS TECHNIQUE IS SIMILAR TO REMBRANDT WARE

A SELECTION OF REMBRANDT POTTERY FROM A DOULTON CATALOGUE SHOWING THE ORIGINAL METAL STANDS AND COVERS, FEW OF WHICH NOW SURVIVE. REMBRANDT WARE WAS INTRODUCED c. 1898 AND WAS SO CALLED AS MANY EXAMPLES DEPICTED REMBRANDT'S PAINTINGS. THE ROUGH TEXTURED BODY WAS COMPOSED OF LOCAL MARLS AND COLOURED WITH SLIPS IN SHADES OF BROWN, OCHRE AND BLACK

A PORCELAIN VASE WITH GILDED HANDLES AND RIM AND RURAL SCENE PAINTED IN SOFT COLOURS BY H ALLEN, c. 1912

By the 1830s, the revival of interest in the formal gardens that had been launched by the Neo-Classical movement had become a popular fashion. Anticipating the likely demand for garden ornaments from the middle classes, Henry Doulton began to make terracotta during the 1830s. Female figures, discreetly erotic beneath classical draperies, garden urns and flower pots, pedestals and balustrades became regular features of the Doulton catalogues. At first, all these and many other garden ornaments were conceived in Classical taste, but gradually they began to reflect all the contemporary vogues for Gothic, naturalist, Renaissance, Japanese, Aesthetic and later Art Nouveau styles. The range was enlarged to include sundials, window boxes, jardinières, garden seats and even garden edging, and many designs could be ordered in both terracotta and coloured stoneware. Brightly coloured majolica glazed wares were also made between 1875 and 1910.

Fountains for conservatories, gardens and parks were designed for production in all these materials. Many of these, designed for domestic settings, were modelled by George

DOULTON LAMBETH

THE GARDEN

Tinworth, and produced in large numbers over a long period. Mostly small in scale, these contrast with Tinworth's better known architectural and exhibition fountains. Arthur Pearce and other Lambeth artists tended to concentrate on the design of wall and drinking fountains, for use in parks, schools and other public settings.

By the late 19th century it was possible to assemble the most elaborate garden schemes from Doulton catalogues, equally suitable

for a stately home or suburban villa. Many important public parks, in London and other new industrial cities, were richly ornamented by Doulton terracotta and stoneware.

After the First World War, Doulton's garden wares reflected the diminished scale and more intimate nature of both public and domestic horticulture. Conservatory fountains and statuary gave way to bird baths and ornamental gnomes and animals, some of which were modelled by well-known Doulton artists such as Mark Marshall and Harry Simeon. While some of these garden ornaments were in questionable taste, others were designed for production by leading Academic sculptors of the period. Examples of the latter were included in the Garden Exhibition held on the roof of Selfridges in 1930, one of a number of exhibitions of the period designed to demonstrate how established artists could improve industrial design. One of the most important sculptors to feature in the Selfridge's exhibition was Gilbert Bayes who was to revolutionise Doulton's production of garden ornaments.

A PAGE FROM A DOULTON CATALOGUE, 1880, SHOWING STONEWARE SEATS, FLOWER POTS AND OTHER GARDEN ORNAMENTS

A GREY TERRACOTTA FIGURE OF A PIXIE DESIGNED BY H SIMEON. THIS WAS ONE OF A RANGE ILLUSTRATED IN A CATALOGUE DATING FROM THE 1920s

A RANGE OF GARDEN EDGING FROM A DOULTON CATALOGUE, 1880. THIS WAS PRODUCED IN BOTH STONEWARE AND TERRACOTTA

A FOUNTAIN IN STONEWARE
DEPICTING INCIDENTS IN THE
BIBLE CONNECTED WITH WATER,
MODELLED IN HIGH RELIEF BY
GEORGE TINWORTH. THIS WAS
FIRST EXHIBITED AT THE PARIS
EXHIBITION OF 1878 AND
THEREAFTER AT THE
WORCESTERSHIRE EXHIBITION,
1882, WHERE THIS PHOTOGRAPH
WAS TAKEN

A PAGE FROM A DOULTON
CATALOGUE, 1910, SHOWING
CONSERVATORY AND WALL
FOUNTAINS, MANY OF WHICH
WERE DESIGNED BY A E PEARCE

A TERRACOTTA GARDEN FIGURE
CALLED *TRUTH*, MODELLED BY
JOHN BROAD, c.1890. MANY FIGURES SUCH
AS THIS WERE DESIGNED BY DOULTON
MODELLERS FOR
GARDEN SETTINGS AND FEATURE IN
THEIR CATALOGUES FROM 1840 UNTIL
1910. OTHER ARTISTS
INCLUDE ARTHUR BEERE,
HERBERT ELLIS AND J B HARDING

Doulton's contribution to the decoration of exteriors and gardens during the 1920s and 1930s was greatly influenced by Gilbert Bayes, the distinguished academic sculptor. From 1923 to 1939 there was a long and valuable relationship between them which resulted in a number of sculptures for architectural or domestic use. These were all made at Lambeth in Polychrome Stoneware, a material much favoured by Bayes because of its colourful and durable properties.

During his long career, Bayes modelled many decorative fountains and garden figures. These not only satisfied his fanciful imagination, but also his social conscience for he felt strongly that decorative sculpture had a role to play in improving the environment. These ideals lead him to collaborate on the production of ex-

GILBERT BAYES

A FOUNTAIN IN POLYCHROME STONEWARE, 1924, IN ITS ORIGINAL GARDEN SETTING. IT WAS EXHIBITED SEVERAL TIMES IN THIS COUNTRY AND ABROAD, IN

tensive garden schemes for a number of housing estates, where the introduction of coloured sculpture could be a source of continual pleasure for the inhabitants.

Bayes' ceramic sculptures were also very suitable for the decoration of a private garden or courtyard, where they could express his own interests in garden design. As a result, he and Doulton produced a number of complete schemes which included playing fountains, decorative roundels and masks and a variety of incidental figures and animals suitable for an intimate garden setting.

Further details about Bayes' architectural work can be found in the Architecture Section at the end of this book.

PARTICULAR AT THE PARIS EXHIBITION 1925 WHERE BAYES WON A GOLD MEDAL AND A DIPLOMA OF HONOUR. A SIMILAR FOUNTAIN WAS DESIGNED FOR THE INTERNATIONAL LABOUR OFFICES, GENEVA

A GROUP OF POLYCHROME STONEWARE SCULPTURES WHICH WERE USED AS FINIALS FOR WASHING LINE POSTS AT ST PANCRAS HOUSING ASSOCIATION ESTATES, AND ALSO AS GARDEN ORNAMENTS. THESE SCULPTURES FEATURED IN EXHIBITIONS AROUND THE COUNTRY AND ABROAD FROM 1936 UNTIL 1939

A MERMAID GARDEN FIGURE IN POLYCHROME STONEWARE, 1937. IT WAS EXHIBITED AT THE LONDON SOCIETY OF ARTS IN 1938 AND ELSEWHERE; VERSIONS COULD BE BOUGHT FOR 60 GUINEAS

Although it is usual to judge any major commercial pottery like Doulton on the basis of the art and studio wares, the exhibition pieces and other items of particularly artistic interest, any such judgement can be misleading. The reputation, and indeed the financial stability of Doulton was founded, not on the pieces that are most sought after today by public and private collectors, but on the many ranges of mass-produced tablewares and ornaments that supplied the bread and butter for the factories and their employees.

Some of these wares are insignificant, while others are actually of historical or aesthetic interest. They are also an invaluable mirror of changing public fashion. These wares have been displayed in the rather fanciful setting of two china shops, one dating from about 1910, the other from the mid 1930s. These dates have been chosen both to mark important periods in the Doulton story and to demonstrate changes in popular taste.

THE EDWARDIAN CHINA SHOP

A TEAPOT AND PLATE DECORATED WITH
THE *BLUE CHILDREN* PATTERN,
PRODUCED AT BURSLEM FROM THE LATE
1880s UNTIL 1928. THIS DESIGN WAS A
MIXTURE OF
PRINTING AND HAND PAINTING

A RANGE OF SERIES WARE RACK PLATES,
FROM THE MANY DESIGNS PRODUCED AT
BURSLEM BETWEEN 1900 AND THE
PRESENT DAY

AN EARTHENWARE EWER AND BASIN
DECORATED WITH THE *NIGHTWATCHMAN*
PATTERN, BURSLEM, c. 1910

PIECES FROM A TEA SERVICE WITH
RAISED GOLD DECORATION, BURSLEM,
c. 1906.
HIGH-QUALITY TABLEWARES OF THIS
TYPE WERE PRODUCED BETWEEN ABOUT
1890 AND THE 1950s

THE 1930's CHINA SHOP

A BURSLEM PUBLICITY
PHOTOGRAPH OF THE 1930s
SHOWING THE *TANGO* TABLEWARE
DESIGN AND THE FIGURE,
CLOTHILDE

A GROUP OF BURSLEM BIRD
MODELS PART OF AN EXTENSIVE RANGE
OF ANIMAL AND BIRDS
MADE FROM THE 1920s UNTIL THE
PRESENT DAY

A PAGE FROM A DOULTON
CATALOGUE OF THE MID 1920s
SHOWING THE *BLUE PERSIAN*
EARTHENWARE PATTERN, MADE
BETWEEN 1917 AND 1942, AND *BIRD OF
PARADISE*, 1922–35. THIS DESIGN WAS ONE
OF A NUMBER ALSO
PRODUCED ON THE TITIANIAN
BODY

A GROUP OF SERIES WARE RACK PLATES,
SOME WITH
BLOCK-PRINTED DESIGNS

ROYAL
DOULTON

"BINYON" D 5461.
Dinner Set, 26 pcs. (6 persons) ... 57/-
... 54 ... (12 persons) ... 109/-
Teaset, 21 pcs. (6 persons) ... 19:9

"ATHLONE" D 5551 Brown, D 5552 Green
Dinner Set, 26 pcs. (6 persons) ... 65/6
... 54 ... (12 persons) ... 125/-
Teaset, 21 pcs. (6 persons) ... 21/-

"NERISSA" D 5590
Dinner Set, 26 pcs. (6 persons) ... 67/6
... 54 ... (12 persons) ... 130/-
Teaset, 21 pcs. (6 persons) ... 22/-

"SCALA" D 5593
Dinner Set, 26 pcs. (6 persons) ... 67/6
... 54 ... (12 persons) ... 130/-

These modern designs can be
supplied in every article used
for table services and sets of
any composition. The prices
are such that "Doulton,"
whilst a luxury to use, is an
economy to buy.

A PORCELAIN VASE WITH
MODERNIST DECORATION IN
BRIGHT COLOURS, BURSLEM, c. 1930

A GROUP OF BURSLEM FIGURES OF THE
1930s, TOP, FROM LEFT TO
RIGHT: *HUNTS LADY, THE BATHER,
GLORIA;* BOTTOM: *SUNSHINE GIRL,
SIESTA, SCOTTIES*

TWO EMBOSSED BURSLEM JUGS, ON THE
LEFT PRINTED WITH THE
JACKDAW OF RHEIMS DESIGN, ON THE
RIGHT ONE FROM A DICKENS RANGE,
c. 1935

A LAMBETH PUBLICITY
PHOTOGRAPH SHOWING A GROUP OF
STONEWARE CONTAINERS FOR FLORAL
DISPLAYS, c. 1930–56

Art Nouveau, which took root in England during the 1890s, inspired many Burslem and Lambeth artists to produce some of the most dynamic and adventurous work to emerge from the Doulton factories. This style, with its lively combination of naturalistic, oriental and other historical elements revolutionised the applied arts and was particularly suitable for the design and decoration of ceramics. The familiar curvilinear, organic forms, the sinuous ladies and other popular symbols such as the lily and the peacock frequently appeared on Doulton products. In some cases the Doulton wares simply reflected the current vogue which underlined the transition from Japanism to Art Nouveau. However, some artists, notably Mark Marshall, Frank Butler, Frank Pope, and Margaret Thompson completely captured the spirit of this dynamic new style. As well as their individual pieces, these artists were also responsible for many designs produced in considerable quantities. In the 1880s Doulton had introduced, at Lambeth, a range of slip-cast wares made in editions of about a thousand which were designed to cater for a wider market. The demand for these modestly priced wares increased greatly during the early 20th century as both the flowing continental styles and the rectilinear and formal designs associated with Scotland and Vienna could be effectively expressed on these pieces. Amongst the best known is the range specially produced for Liberty's.

The effect of Art Nouveau was considerable and long-lasting. At Burslem, it could be seen in its more extreme form in the Morrisian Wares but it was reflected generally in the porcelain and Titanian ornamental wares which assumed more elongated and mannered shapes. The painted decoration by artists such as Harry Allen, Harry Tittensor and Edward Raby also showed its influence. Several stylish pieces were directly inspired by the distinctive, elegant Dutch and Belgian Art Nouveau ceramics, in particular Rozenburg.

The New Style achieved popular expression on a wide range of tablewares, from richly-decorated porcelains to basic earthenwares. Only the outbreak of war effectively brought the Art Nouveau style to a close, by which time its decorative and sensual extremes had in any case frequently lost their vitality. The new age that dawned after the First World War was keen to eradicate the styles and trends of the previous generation.

ART NOUVEAU

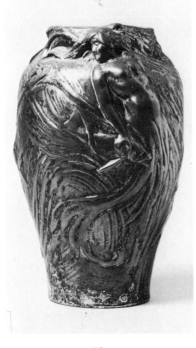

A BUFF STONEWARE VASE MODELLED IN RELIEF WITH METALLIC BRONZE FINISH BY FRANCIS POPE, LAMBETH, c. 1905. THIS EFFECT WAS ACHIEVED BY AN ELECTROPLATING PROCESS

A MIRROR FRAME IN BROWN STONEWARE BY GEORGE TINWORTH, LAMBETH, c. 1905

A LARGE, RICHLY-COLOURED FAIENCE PLAQUE BY JOHN McLENNAN, LAMBETH, c. 1895

AN EARTHENWARE MOONFLASK
DECORATED WITH PRINTED DECORATION
IN THE JAPANESE AESTHETIC STYLE,
BURSLEM, c. 1890

AN ADVERTISEMENT FROM A DOULTON
CATALOGUE ILLUSTRATING A SELECTION
OF SLIP-CAST AND PAINTED VASES WHICH
WERE DESIGNED FOR REPRODUCTION IN
LARGE EDITIONS BY W ROWE,
L HARRADINE, M MARSHALL,
M E THOMPSON, F POPE AND OTHERS,
LAMBETH, 1910–25

A PORCELAIN TEA SERVICE WITH FLORAL
DECORATION IN AN ART NOUVEAU STYLE,
BURSLEM, c. 1905

A PORCELAIN VASE PAINTED IN PASTEL
SHADES IN A DUTCH ART NOUVEAU
STYLE, BURSLEM, 1912

AN EARTHENWARE VASE AND COVER,
THE INCISED ART NOUVEAU DESIGN
DECORATED WITH RAISED SLIP AND
GOLD, BURSLEM, c. 1905

A JARDINIÈRE IN MORRISIAN WARE
PRINTED WITH A DESIGN IN BLACK AND
YELLOW, IN THE STYLE OF THE
AMERICAN ILLUSTRATOR WILL BRADLEY,
c. 1910.
MORRISIAN WARE WAS IN PRODUCTION
AT BURSLEM FROM 1900 UNTIL 1924; THE
UNUSUAL NAME WAS PROBABLY A
TRIBUTE TO WILLIAM MORRIS

During the 1930s the Council for Art and Industry promoted a series of exhibitions designed to show the contribution to commercial design made by contemporary artists and sculptors. This reflected the considerable public concern about the state of the relationship between art and industry. Doulton was inevitably affected, but it already had a fairly progressive outlook towards design at this time and had close connections with several established artists and designers outside the ceramic industry. Encouraged by enlightened art directors, C J Noke and J H Mott, a number of artists were able to make important contributions to both Lambeth and Burslem production. It would appear that contact was made either by word of mouth, through organisations like the Art Workers Guild or, through exhibitions at the Royal Academy and other galleries.

Frank Brangwyn (1867–1956), who had already worked as a designer of furniture, textiles and ceramics, produced a number of designs for Doulton of tableware and ornaments. These very original conceptions were acclaimed by contemporary critics who admired their shape, their painterly decoration and their modest prices. However they were not successful commercially.

Richard Garbe (1876–1957), Professor of Sculpture at the Royal College of Art, modelled a number of figures,

Designed by F. Brangwyn R.A

ART AND INDUSTRY

A PORCELAIN WALLMASK WITH A TURQUOISE GLAZE TITLED *ST AGNES*, DESIGNED BY RICHARD GARBE. THIS WAS PRODUCED IN A LIMITED EDITION AT BURSLEM, 1934

wall masks and other wares for reproduction in limited editions at both the Burslem and Lambeth factories. Some of these were based on his existing sculptures in stone or ivory, while others appear to have been specially designed for Doulton. The work of other academic sculptors such as David Evans, Allan Howes, Adrian Allinson, and George Paulin was also reproduced in ceramic form by Doulton.

Reco Capey (1895–1961), Professor of Design at the Royal College of Art, worked at Lambeth for a period, producing a number of unusual stoneware pieces, including oven ware. These at first were marketed by Doulton, apparently with little success, and the later wares were sold through his agent and did not carry Doulton marks.

At the same time, many of the artists and designers employed by Doulton, such as Vera Huggins, Harry Simeon and Doris Johnson produced some very stylish work. This reflected not only the influence of the outside artists, but also an awareness of the new styles of pottery emerging from the studios of Bernard Leach, William Staite Murray and others. Doulton artists were able to adapt hand-throwing and earthy glazes for industrial production, and so produced some of the best designed and executed ceramics of the period.

A PAIR OF BOOKENDS IN THE FORM OF RAMS IN MOTTLED GLAZED STONEWARE DESIGNED BY H SIMEON, LAMBETH, c. 1925

A PILGRIM FLASK IN BUFF
STONEWARE MODELLED IN RELIEF AND
DEPICTING *ENDYMION AND
AURORA* BY RICHARD GARBE,
LAMBETH, 1934

A FIGURE IN WHITE GLAZED
EARTHENWARE DEPICTING *DIANA*,
DESIGNED BY DAVID EVANS AND MADE
AT BURSLEM IN 1928. THIS FIGURE WAS
ADAPTED FROM A
SMALLER BRONZE OF THE SAME
SUBJECT WHICH WAS EXHIBITED AT THE
ROYAL ACADEMY

THE CLOUD, A CAST PORCELAIN
FIGURE DESIGNED BY
RICHARD GARBE FOR LIMITED
PRODUCTION AT BURSLEM IN 1937

A STONEWARE VASE AND COVER WITH
RICH BLUE GLAZE TRICKLING OVER A
BUFF GROUND BY
V HUGGINS, LAMBETH, c. 1935

A LAMBETH PUBLICITY PHOTOGRAPH FROM THE MID 1930s SHOWING AN EARTHENWARE PLAQUE BY H SIMEON AND A STONEWARE VASE BY V HUGGINS. SIMILAR PIECES ARE INCLUDED IN THE EXHIBITION

A SELECTION OF PIECES FROM AN EARTHENWARE TEA SERVICE IN THE *HARVEST* PATTERN DESIGNED BY FRANK BRANGWYN AND MADE AT BURSLEM FROM 1930 UNTIL 1940

Many of Doulton's earliest products were made for brewers, distillers and publicans, a trading association that flourished for over a hundred years. Stoneware barrels, bottles, spirit flasks and jugs were produced in vast quantities at Lambeth over a long period; many of these were impressed with either the name of the brewer or the details of the public house or retailer who was going to sell them.

The Victorian public house was a structure of unparalleled splendour, decorated inside and out with glittering glass, gleaming metalwork, and ceramic-clad walls which were both attractive and hygienic. Doulton was responsible for the decoration of many public houses, facing the outside with their coloured stoneware and Carraraware, and enriching the inside with faience and large tile murals. They also produced much of the furniture and equipment, including spittoons, beer-engine handles, tankards, decanters, tobacco jars,

THE PUBLIC HOUSE

A SELECTION OF KINGSWARE MADE AT BURSLEM BETWEEN 1900 AND 1939. THESE SLIP-DECORATED EARTHENWARES WERE FREQUENTLY USED TO ADVERTISE DEWAR'S WHISKY

match strikers, and ash trays. Many of these were used as advertising vehicles by brewers and distillers, and were decorated with trade-marks and slogans. Initially, standard shapes were used, but later more ambitious advertising pieces were specially designed for production at Lambeth and Burslem. Best known is the wide range produced for Dewar's; other interesting pieces include the Sandeman and Jim Crow bottles, the Bell's flask in the shape of a bell and the ash tray made for Silver Seal port. Other Doulton products, although not designed specifically for the public house, have tended to be associated with them and their decoration. These include the simulated copper and leather ware, made at Lambeth, the range of colourful Toby wares produced at Lambeth during the 1920s and at Burslem ten years later, and the popular Character Jug range, introduced at Burslem in 1934, and still in production.

A SELECTION OF JUGS AND
GOBLETS IN COPPER AND BLACK
LEATHER WARE MADE AT
LAMBETH FROM c. 1887 UNTIL 1914.
COPPERWARE WAS PRODUCED BY
PAINTING A SILICON BODY WITH A
COPPER LUSTRE GLAZE AND
ADDING SIMULATED JOINTS AND
RIVETS. BLACK LEATHER WARE
WAS ALSO MADE FROM A SILICON BODY,
GLAZED BLACK WITH MOCK STITCHING.
ALSO INCLUDED IN
THIS RANGE WERE HAMMERED
COPPER AND CAST IRON
IMITATIONS

A FLASK IN THE FORM OF A CROW MADE
FOR OLD CROW BOURBON, NATIONAL
DISTILLERS, KENTUCKY, BURSLEM, 1954

A PAGE FROM A DOULTON CATALOGUE OF 1927 ADVERTISING THE RANGE OF STONEWARE JUGS, TOBACCO JARS AND INK POTS MODELLED IN THE FORM OF TOBY FIGURES. THESE WERE DESIGNED BY H SIMEON AND PRODUCED AT LAMBETH BETWEEN 1924 AND 1939.

TWO STONEWARE ADVERTISING NOVELTIES MADE AT LAMBETH, c. 1910, THE BOOK HIP FLASK FOR DEWAR'S AND THE ASH TRAY FOR SILVER SEAL PORT

OLD CHARLEY, ONE OF A RANGE OF CHARACTER JUGS FIRST PRODUCED AT BURSLEM IN 1934

Doulton's interest in the nursery dates from the late 19th century when the range of utilitarian products made at Lambeth included feeders, small-scale hot-water bottles, breast warmers and other equally obscure Victorian devices. Water filters, a standard piece of domestic equipment, were specially decorated with images suitable for children's rooms. This reflects the contemporary concern for child health. Special children's hospitals were founded around the turn of the century and many of these had tile panels depicting nursery rhymes to amuse the young patients. Margaret Thompson and William Rowe were responsible for the designs of these panels which were installed in hospitals in this country and abroad.

As well as their various child-care products, Doulton made wares designed to appeal specifically to children themselves, such as stoneware money boxes, and whistles in the shape of dogs. A variety of miniature stoneware jugs, mugs and other pieces were also produced as toys and furnishings for doll's houses.

Several ranges of tableware were specially designed for children at the

THE NURSERY

Burslem factory from 1900 onwards 'Alice in Wonderland' featured on one of the earliest ranges and there were also several nursery rhyme series; one of these was adapted from illustrations by William Savage Cooper

A SELECTION OF PIECES DECORATED WITH SCENES FROM *ALICE IN WONDERLAND*, IN PRODUCTION AT BURSLEM FROM 1906 UNTIL 1932. THE DESIGNER IS NOT RECORDED

(1863–1943) a frequent exhibitor at the Royal Academy. These designs were also used on biscuit caskets for Huntley and Palmers nursery rhyme biscuits.

Apart from the Series Wares there were many items decorated individually, for example the familiar thick-sided baby plate with a Cecil Aldin dog design, or mugs with relief decoration of chickens, ducks and squirrels.

The range most commonly associated with Doulton is the Bunnykins series, first introduced in 1934. This whimsical rabbit family was originally the creation of Barbara Vernon, who has spent her life in a convent. Her drawings launched the range, and since then over 150 designs have appeared, many of which are still in production. The Bunnykins range has also included figures but, of course, many other figure and animal models, although not specifically designed for the young market, have become well-established children's favourites. Similarly bibelots and other fancies made originally for adults now have a wide appeal for children.

A PLATE FROM A RANGE DECORATED
WITH NURSERY RHYMES. INCLUDED IN
THE
SERIES WAS A CASKET ADOPTED BY
HUNTLEY AND PALMERS AS AN
ADVERTISING PIECE. W SAVAGE COOPER,
A PAINTER WHO EXHIBITED AT THE
ROYAL ACADEMY, WAS RESPONSIBLE FOR
THE
DESIGNS WHICH WERE IN PRODUCTION AT
BURSLEM FROM 1903 UNTIL 1936

A BABY HOT WATER BOTTLE IN MOTTLED
BLUE-GREEN STONEWARE WITH APPLIED
RELIEFS, LAMBETH, c. 1910

A NURSERY-RHYME TILE PANEL
DEPICTING *MARY, MARY, QUITE
CONTRARY,*
DESIGNED BY M E THOMPSON FOR A
CHILDREN'S WARD AT UNIVERSITY
COLLEGE HOSPITAL, LONDON, c. 1900

A PAGE FROM A DOULTON CATALOGUE
SHOWING STONEWARE FILTERS
INCLUDING ONE SPECIALLY DESIGNED
FOR THE NURSERY, LAMBETH, c. 1910

A SELECTION OF PIECES FROM A SERVICE
DECORATED WITH NURSERY RHYMES,
BURSLEM, 1920. THE DESIGNER IS NOT
RECORDED

A SELECTION OF WATER COLOUR DESIGNS
FOR BUNNYKINS WARE BY
BARBARA VERNON, c. 1936

A GROUP OF CHILDREN FIGURES. FROM
LEFT TO RIGHT: *WEE WILLIE WINKIE,
ANNETTE, LITTLE LADY MAKE-BELIEVE,
HERE A LITTLE CHILD I STAND* AND *MY
TEDDY*, BURSLEM, 1930–55

At the beginning of this century drawings by a number of popular graphic artists were reproduced on Doulton products. In 1900, Doulton were given the chance of issuing a series of rack plates decorated with the satyrical cartoons of Charles Dana Gibson (1867–1944). These 24 cartoons featured the life and times of his famous 'Gibson Girl', an Edwardian beauty whose activities lampooned the social life of the elite of the period. The popularity of the 'Gibson Girl' had already reached cult proportions, particularly in America, and so Doulton's success was assured. A further series then followed, decorated with Gibson Girl heads, the pin-ups of the period; Doulton also reproduced some Gibson golfing cartoons.

C J Noke was quick to realise the potential offered by popular illustrators, and so acquired the rights to reproduce a number of other series. David H Souter, (1862–1935), a friend and colleague of Phil May, was well known in Australia for his decorative Art Nouveau drawings of cats. A

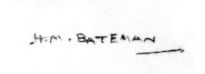

POPULAR ILLUSTRATORS

range of Souter drawings, as well as actual models of his comic cats, were reproduced at Burslem. Another rack plate series was based on the cartoons of Randolph Caldecott (1846–86), probably the best-known graphic artist of the period. Cecil Aldin (1870–1935) is remembered for his book illustrations and travel posters;

his humorous hunting scenes and comic dog series were effectively used by Doulton on a range of Burslem products. H M Bateman (1887–1970), the popular social satyrist, contributed a range of humorous drawings of his familiar 'types' which included the frustrated golfer and other well-known characters.

Most of these popular ranges were made at Burslem, but there is at least one well-known artist associated with Lambeth. John Hassall (1868–1948) supplied a series of simple and amusing designs which were reproduced on a number of stoneware jugs, mugs, candlesticks and other items. However, the quantities produced were inevitably far smaller than the Burslem Series Wares. Although none of these artists achieved the cult following associated with Gibson, their popularity ensured a good sale for Doulton items decorated with their designs. It is therefore surprising that Doulton was one of the few potteries to exploit extensively this area of the market.

A WALLPAPER DESIGN BY CHARLES DANA GIBSON 'SUITABLE FOR A BACHELOR'S APARTMENT'. SIMILAR GIBSON GIRL HEADS WERE LATER APPLIED TO A SET OF TWELVE DOULTON PLATES, INTRODUCED AT BURSLEM IN 1901

TWO SMALL VASES DECORATED WITH PRINTED GOLFING CARTOONS BY C D GIBSON, FROM A SERIES INTRODUCED AT BURSLEM IN 1905

A DOULTON PUBLICITY PHOTOGRAPH
SHOWING THE RANGE OF WARES
DECORATED WITH CARTOONS BY
HENRY MAYO BATEMAN, MADE AT
BURSLEM 1937–50

TWO DESIGNS FROM A RANGE BY DAVID
HENRY SOUTER. THE PLATE, PRINTED
WITH COMIC CATS, WAS MADE AT
BURSLEM
BETWEEN 1906 AND 1939; THE CAT MODEL
REPRESENTING SOUTER'S CHARACTER
KATEROO WAS MADE AT BURSLEM c. 1912

A PLATE WITH A PRINTED DECORATION
BASED ON A CARTOON *THE YOUNG FOLKS*
BY RANDOLPH CALDECOTT, BURSLEM,
1908

A MUG WITH A GOLFING CARTOON FROM
THE BATEMAN RANGE

A BROWN STONEWARE JUG WITH A
PRINTED CARTOON BY JOHN HASSALL,
ONE OF A RANGE OF DESIGNS PRODUCED
AT LAMBETH c. 1910

A TEAPOT AND A PLATE WITH PRINTED
DESIGNS OF OLD ENGLISH SCENES BY
CECIL ALDIN, 1926 ALDIN'S DESIGNS OF
COMIC DOGS WERE ALSO USED ON A
SERIES OF DOULTON PLATES

Both the Lambeth and Burslem factories specialised in a small way in the production of items to be used for advertising purposes. Until the development of plastics, ceramics were the ideal promotional material, being attractive, durable, easy to produce, cheap and hygienic. The brewers and distillers were Doulton's major clients in this field, and many of their advertising wares are shown in the section devoted to the Public House. Other clients included those who manufactured or sold such diverse products as toothpaste, tea, biscuits, cigarettes, electrical components, bricks, spare parts for cars, soap, perfume and loudspeakers. Many of Doulton's standard ranges of plates, ashtrays, bottles and jugs were adapted for advertising purposes by the addition of a trade-mark, symbol, motto or other relevant decoration. These pieces inevitably form the bulk of the advertising wares. Some companies, however, did commission

ADVERTISING WARES

special designs, which took the form of figures, animal models, candlesticks and even model tugboats. Among these, some are really quite bizarre, for example the feet produced for Dr Scholl, or the Toby Jug model

of the American industrialist Cliff Cornell. Others reveal the changing standards of advertising; in 1897 it was perfectly acceptable for Vinolia Soap to use a portrait of Queen Victoria to advertise their product.

Ordinary tablewares often carried advertising slogan or images. Fry's Cocoa, for instance, appeared on cups and saucers. Closely related to these are the badged wares specially made for restaurants, hotels, shipping companies, railways, and other similar organisations. The production of these items has always been, and still is, a major part of Doulton output.

Doulton naturally used their ingenuity and experience in the field to advertise their own products. Miniature barrels, hot-water bottles, drain pipes, lavatories, wash basins and even crucibles were made in large numbers and used as travellers' samples to promote their domestic, industrial and sanitary wares.

TABLEWARE DESIGNED FOR THE SAVOY HOTEL, DECORATED WITH A PINK BANDED MOTIF AND A GREY BADGE. A SIMILAR
DESIGN WAS ALSO PRODUCED FOR CLARIDGES. BURSLEM, c.1935

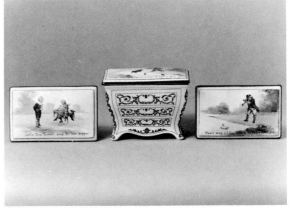

A CASKET AND LIDS DECORATED WITH NURSERY-RHYME SCENES BY W SAVAGE COOPER AND USED AS A BISCUIT BOX BY HUNTLEY AND
PALMERS, 1905. SIMILAR CASKETS WITH NO ADVERTISING
INSCRIPTIONS WERE MADE AT BURSLEM BETWEEN 1903 AND 1914 AS PART OF THE SAVAGE COOPER RANGE

A TOBY JUG DEPICTING
CLIFF CORNELL, THE OWNER OF
THE CLEVELAND FLUX COMPANY, MADE
FOR ADVERTISING PURPOSES AT
BURSLEM IN THE 1950s

A CHINA FIGURE SPECIALLY DESIGNED
AT BURSLEM IN 1923 TO ADVERTISE
GROSSMITH'S PERFUME. YARDLEYS ALSO
USED A DOULTON FIGURE GROUP TO
ADVERTISE THEIR *OLD ENGLISH
LAVENDER* PERFUME, c.1925

A CANDLESTICK IN GREEN GLAZED
STONEWARE, DESIGNED BY
GILBERT BAYES FOR ALLIED
NEWSPAPERS LTD, LAMBETH, 1935

A BONE CHINA PLAQUE WITH A
PRINTED PORTRAIT OF
QUEEN VICTORIA, MADE TO
ADVERTISE VINOLIA SOAP,
BURSLEM, 1897. A SIMILAR PLAQUE
ADVERTISING MOËT CHANDON
CHAMPAGNE WAS DECORATED
WITH A PICTURE OF EDWARD VII

A MODEL OF A FOOT ON A DISPLAY
STAND, ONE OF A RANGE MADE AT
BURSLEM IN THE 1930s FOR
DR SCHOLL PRODUCTS

STONEWARE TUG BOATS AND
BARGES MADE TO ADVERTISE A
NUMBER OF LIGHTERAGE AND
DOCKYARD COMPANIES, LAMBETH, c. 1925

A SELECTION OF GLAZED
STONEWARE ASHTRAYS AND
FLOWER VASES DESIGNED FOR THE
ORIENT LINE SHIPPING COMPANY,
LAMBETH, 1950. DOULTONS ALSO
DESIGNED BADGED WARE FOR THE
CUNARD LINE

Henry Doulton was one of the first to realise the full implications of the sanitary revolution that was under way by the 1840s. Standards of public health and hygiene had been low for centuries but the spread of industrialisation during the late 18th and early 19th centuries had caused a rapid decline. Cholera and similar diseases were increasingly common in London and other major cities, and so public pressure upon the Government to control the situation mounted.

Much of this pressure was directed by Edwin Chadwick who was to earn the title, 'The Father of Sanitary Science'. Chadwick, an opinionated and rather egoistic character, was instrumental in persuading Henry Doulton to enter the field of sanitary production, having convinced him in 1845, with the help of Doulton's friends the Engineering Inspectors Edward Cresy and Robert Rawlinson, that the stoneware pipe would be the basis of the sanitary revolution. Doulton decided to open a special factory at Lambeth in 1845 to concentrate on the production of stoneware pipes. The success of this factory, and the increasing demand for sanitary pipes led to the opening of additional factories, at St Helens in 1847, and at Dudley in 1848.

Also in 1848, the passing of the Public Health Act not only firmly underlined Chadwick's foresight but ensured that the production of sanitary products was to remain the basis for Doulton fortunes for many years to come. In 1854, *The Builder* was able to state: 'Messrs Doulton estimate that they manufacture one fifth of the pipe sewers made throughout the country and they manufacture at the rate of ten miles of sewer a week!' From the 1880s until the late 1930s Doulton stoneware pipes were also exported all over the world.

The Doulton involvement in sanitary production spread rapidly beyond stoneware pipes, and by the 1870s the catalogues were filled with all manner of sinks, closets, lavatories, baths and other sanitary

SANITARY AND INDUSTRIAL PRODUCTION

fittings. Water filters and other purification equipment also played an important and long-lasting role. These were made at Lambeth and the other factories initially, but soon spread to new works at Burslem, Paisley and elsewhere.

One of Henry Doulton's reasons for buying a share in the Burslem factory of Pinder Bourne & Co was that Company's established interests in sanitary and industrial production.

THE DISPLAY OF INDUSTRIAL AND SANITARY WARES AT THE CHICAGO EXHIBITION, 1893

The Paisley Works was established in 1888, primarily for the production of cast iron baths and other sanitary metalware.

The range of Doulton sanitary production was quite staggering and included both the basic wares required for hospital, prison and ship use as well as the splendidly opulent, such as those fitted in the Reform Club, Manchester.

In 1901, Doulton's important contribution to sanitary science was acknowledged with the award of a Royal Warrant, a propitious start to their 20th century production. In the opening decades of this century they secured the largest and most prestigious sanitary contracts. Included amongst these were those for County Hall and the Savoy Hotel, London, the latter necessitating the production of 237 specially designed baths. Commissions for overseas work increased at this period, in particular in India, where they installed sanitary systems in a number of palaces and other official residences.

In the 1930s re-organisation led to the concentration of production at Stoke and Lambeth. The Paisley factory was sold in 1936, and in 1937 production at Nile Street ceased, having been moved to the newly acquired Whieldon Sanitary Potteries. This factory, still the headquarters of Doulton sanitaryware, has in turn expanded by further mergers, in 1945 with Arthur Winkle Ltd, and in 1969 with Johnson & Slater. In the meantime, stoneware production at Lambeth had ceased, and vitreous china had replaced earthenware at the other factories. Finally, in 1974, Doulton Sanitaryware became a European company from its partnership with Keramag of Germany and Allia of France. Today, acrylic baths and other new technological developments have replaced the stoneware sewer pipes but these still maintain the tradition established in 1845 by Henry Doulton.

No less significant has been the

Doulton involvement in industrial ceramics. As early as 1818 Doulton & Watts were producing retorts, equipment and storage vessels for the chemical industry, including a wide range of condensers. By the middle of the century storage vessels to hold up to 500 gallons were in production, fired in special large kilns. Many of these chemical wares were shown at the Great Exhibition of 1851. In 1863 Doulton began the manufacture of plumbago crucibles for muffle, smelting and other furnaces for use in the metal, glass and jewellery trades. The demand for these speceal heat and acid resistant wares continued to grow, keeping pace with new technologies of the period. Components for pumps, pressure vessels, accumulators and batteries, and for the new photographic industry were added to the range, which probably reached its peak during the First World War. At this time the demands from the armaments, explosives and other war industries were considerable, and yet Doulton still found time to develop a type of refractory porcelain to replace the wares that hitherto had been imported from Germany. Crucibles and other

chemical wares remained in production at Lambeth until the 1930s, and then the manufacture switched to the Midlands after the purchase of the old established works of George Shey & Co at Wilmcote. The production of chemical stonewares was finally discontinued in 1964.

Henry Doulton also developed an early interest in the electrical industry, and by the 1850s had turned his attention to the production of

PAGES FROM A DOULTON CATALOGUE,
1898

insulators, in stoneware and earthenware. The company supplied some of the earliest insulators used by the Great Western Railway for its electric telegraph and by the 1880s were making a wide range for the transport, telephone and power industries. The development of electric power also encouraged Doulton to manufacture a range of conduits for underground cables, some of which were developed and patented by Doulton themselves. After the 1920s many of the conduits were produced at the Erith Pipe Works, while the production of insulators had also begun to be moved from Lambeth to the Midlands during the same period. Reorganisation of the company after the closure of Lambeth in 1956 finally separated industrial ceramics from other areas of production. Today the two Doulton industrial companies, Doulton Industrial Products Limited, situated at Stone, and the Tamworth-based Doulton Insulators Limited continue the manufacture of electrical porcelains and specialised ceramics for the engineering, textile, aerospace and other industries.

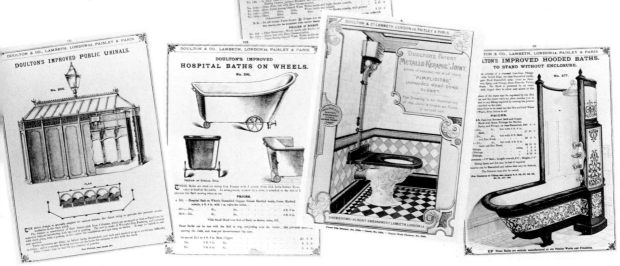

A RANGE OF CHEMICAL
STONEWARE VESSELS

A CATALOGUE PAGE, 1890

STONEWARE CONDUITS FOR ELECTRICITY
CABLES BEING LAID, 1910

A CATALOGUE PAGE, c. 1890

TWO PAGES FROM A DOULTON PUBLICITY
BOOK OF 1925 SHOWING INSULATORS AND
CRUCIBLES

During the late 1890s, C J Noke began to experiment with the production of high-temperature transmutation glazes, in order to recreate some of the oriental techniques of the past. These experiments were given a boost in 1900 when Cuthbert Bailey joined Doulton, as he was particularly interested in the chemistry of these exotic glaze effects. Bailey was probably instrumental in persuading Bernard Moore to work for Doulton as a consultant, and Moore appears to have given Doulton the benefits of his lengthy experience in this field. They concentrated at first on the *flambé* glazes, and were able to launch the fruits of their experiments on a commercial basis at the St Louis International Exhibition of 1904. Here, and at later displays, such as Brussels 1910, the wares were highly acclaimed; contemporary critics compared them favourably with the Chinese pieces that inspired them, and placed them on a par with similar experimental wares produced at Sèvres, Berlin and Copenhagen. Encouraged by this response, Doulton stepped up their 'studio' production. The *flambé* glazed range was increased to include animal

THE BURSLEM STUDIO

models and other fancies, and wares with landscapes and other scenes painted beneath the glaze. From these wares developed the Sung range, introduced in 1920, which Gordon Forsyth

TWO ELEPHANTS DECORATED WITH *FLAMBÉ* GLAZES MODELLED BY C J NOKE. THESE ARE FROM A RANGE OF ANIMAL MODELS WITH *FLAMBÉ* DECORATION MADE OVER A LONG PERIOD FROM ABOUT 1908

called: 'the very finest effort yet made in the history of English pottery to produce work of high artistic value.' *Flambé* in one form or another has remained in production at Burslem until today.

The crystalline range, another experimental high-temperature ware, was introduced at Burslem in 1907 but eventually had to be withdrawn c. 1914 as the technique, which involved the exploding of metallic crystals in the glaze, was difficult to control and therefore not viable on a commercial scale. The same problems of controlling kiln effects affected the Chinese Jade wares which were only made in limited numbers from 1920 until the 1940s. These were thick creamy glazed pieces coloured to resemble the precious stone. Chang Ware, however, took advantage of the inevitable accidents of the kiln and had a more prolific output from 1925 until the war. On this ware, several layers of thick, richly-coloured glazes were allowed to run at random and react against each other creating a varied crackled surface. Each piece was unique and the quality was far beyond conventional commercial production.

A PORCELAIN VASE WITH RICHLY-COLOURED STREAKY GLAZES. THIS EXPERIMENTAL PIECE, PROBABLY MADE BY CUTHBERT BAILEY, PREDATES COMMERCIAL *FLAMBÉ* PRODUCTION

A LARGE SUNG VASE. DESIGNED BY J C NOKE, c. 1925

PIECES FROM A TEA AND COFFEE SERVICE, DECORATED WITH *FLAMBÉ* GLAZES, WITH SILVER MOUNTS DATED 1906. *FLAMBÉ* TABLEWARES WERE ONLY PRODUCED FOR A SHORT PERIOD BECAUSE OF THE DIFFICULTIES OF MATCHING THE RED COLOUR

A PORCELAIN VASE IN PEACH COLOURS WITH CRYSTALLINE GLAZE EFFECTS, 1912

A CHANG MODEL OF A DRAGON ON A
ROCK, c. 1930

A DOULTON ADVERTISEMENT FOR SUNG
WARE, c.1920

A CHANG VASE WITH PAINTED
DECORATION, c. 1930

A GROUP OF PIECES DECORATED WITH
THE CHINESE JADE
TECHNIQUE, c. 1930

ROYAL DOULTON
OLD SUNG WARE

The outbreak of the First World War effectively brought the Lambeth Studio to a close. Many artists were called up, while others became involved in war work of one kind or another. In any case, there was by then only a limited public interest in decorative art wares in the late Victorian style. When peace finally came, it brought with it a new set of problems. First of all, there was a popular demand for a new kind of bright, decorative, mass-produced pottery, a demand that Lambeth initially found hard to satisfy. Second, the definition of art pottery had been dramatically altered by the new generation of studio potters, who rejected industry outright. Despite this, the Lambeth Studio survived, although on a much reduced scale, under the inspired direction of J H Mott. An excellent glaze chemist, Mott produced a number of experimental pieces with striking oriental glaze effects, rarely seen on stoneware before. Although influenced by similar experiments at Burslem, these pieces are quite original and represent a perfect marriage between the personal artistic statement and industrial technology. Mott also extended the colour range of saltglazed stoneware which enabled artists such as William Rowe and Harry Simeon to create both new style individual studio wares and original designs for quantity production. The range of Persian inspired wares, for instance, gave a new dimension to the studio. By the 1930s the future of the Studio was more assured. More artists were employed and with the emergence of designers such as Vera Huggins and Joan Cowper, it began to echo the emancipated Studio of the Victorian period. Huggins in particular was an artist in the old style, capable of a prodigious output in a great variety of original styles, suitable for both quantity and individual production. Cowper, however, had a more limited output, but she was responsible for both the throwing and the decoration of her works. The work of the Doulton

THE LATE LAMBETH STUDIO

A STONEWARE VASE WITH INCISED AND PAINTED DECORATION BY H SIMEON AND V HUGGINS, c. 1928

artists at this period reflects the current preoccupations of the Studio Pottery movement, the interest in oriental forms and decoration and early English pottery. Their achievements compare favourably with those of Leach, Hamada and Murray; indeed the contemporary press continually classed them and Doulton together.

The Second World War again drastically reduced the staff and status of the Studio. During the war decorative pottery could only be made for export, and unfortunately the export potential of Lambeth stoneware was not great. After the war, the Studio only survived at first because it was responsible for the design and production of the familiar LCC blue plaques and other commemorative panels.

However, in 1952, following the success of the Festival of Britain, it was decided to revitalise the Studio. Agnete Hoy, a Danish potter and designer who had previously directed a similar studio operated by Bullers, a Staffordshire company better known for its electrical porcelain, was persuaded to come to Lambeth and take control of the Studio. With her proven artistic abilities and her familiarity with high-temperature ceramics, Agnete Hoy was able to recreate some of the earlier status of the Studio. Her inspiration was diverse, including European 17th and 18th century ceramics and the currently popular craft traditions of Africa and other primitive cultures. She recruited skilled assistants such as Helen Walters, and built up a department whose products were once again quite distinctive and which were well received by contemporary critics. However this new revival was destined to be short lived. In 1956 the Lambeth factory finally closed, the kilns having been fired for the last time with commemorative pieces designed and made in the Studio. So, after nearly 90 years, a relationship between art and industry unique in the history of English ceramics came to an end.

VERA HUGGINS IN THE STUDIO, c. 1945

A STONEWARE VASE WITH MOTTLED
DARK BROWN GLAZE BY V HUGGINS, c.
1937

A STONEWARE MODEL OF A CAT WITH
INCISED AND PAINTED DECORATION BY
AGNETE HOY, 1954

AGNETE HOY AT WORK AT LAMBETH, c. 1954

A PUBLICITY PHOTOGRAPH SHOWING A GROUP OF INCISED AND PAINTED STONEWARES BY AGNETE HOY, c. 1955

HELEN WALTERS AT WORK AT LAMBETH, 1956

A PUBLICITY PHOTOGRAPH SHOWING A GROUP OF STONEWARE MADE BY HELEN WALTERS, LAMBETH, 1956

This section is designed to give a broader picture of Doulton architectural and sculptural work, and to serve as a guide book for those who wish to study the subject further.

The buildings, tile panels, statues, fountains and other works in the section have been selected as examples of the many varied techniques and styles practised by Doulton. Some are magnificent structures by major architects, with splendid decoration, while others are quite minor, and relevant only for their ceramic details. Taken together, they represent the wide range of Doulton work.

The size of this catalogue has meant that there are many other buildings of Doulton relevance excluded. Equally, there are many others which may be attributed to Doulton, though the necessary documentary evidence is lacking.

The examples have also been selected on a regional basis, to cover as many areas in Britain – and abroad – as possible. The entries are listed first of all in groups relating to their materials and techniques, and then regionally within each group. Each group starts in central London, moves

ARCHITECTURE & SCULPTURE

to outer London, and then to the rest of Britain and overseas.

Each entry includes details of location, the name of architect, artist, designer or sculptor involved, and date. Where available, illustration references are also given.

Books and magazines useful for a further study of Doulton's architectural and sculptural work are included in the booklist.

The manufacture of ceramic materials for architectural purposes was an important part of Doulton activities and one which, to date, has not been fully documented.

Lambeth had a well-established tradition in this field. Towards the close of the 18th century, the Coade family had set up a small factory to make a form of terracotta or Coade stone as their ware was called. This business flourished well into the 19th century producing garden vases, statuary and tombs as well as panels and friezes for the enrichment of buildings. Distinguished sculptors were engaged as modellers and the standard of execution was of a very high quality. Consequently celebrated architects like the Adam brothers, Wyatt and Nash made considerable use of this artificial stone.

Doultons' architectural ceramics department developed from more humble beginnings. In the 1820s, John Doulton started to produce terracotta building components like chimney pots, ridge tiles and also garden urns. It was not until Henry Doulton's artistic aspirations were felt within the pottery in the late 1830s that this

CATALOGUE PAGE SHOWING TERRACOTTA MEDALLIONS BY TINWORTH

CATALOGUE PAGE SHOWING A RANGE OF CHIMNEY POTS

CATALOGUE PAGE SHOWING TERRACOTTA WINDOW

essentially utilitarian range was expanded to include terracotta sculpture.

In this new field of design, Henry Doulton was able to draw upon the expertise and advice of his friend Samuel Nixon, a south London sculptor. A picture of the pottery around 1840 shows their early achievements. The old courtyard is crowded with terracotta figures, most of which were destined to become garden ornaments. Some, however, were specially designed for architectural situations, like the statue of Sir John Crosby modelled by Nixon in 1837 which once stood in front of Crosby Hall. Terracotta relief panels were also produced for the decoration of buildings. One of their earliest commissions was a large coat of arms for a local school.

By 1855, the demand for this type of work had grown sufficiently for Henry Doulton to build a new kiln. John Sparkes, the headmaster of the Lambeth School of Art, was very interested in the progress of this architectural department and, over the years, his efforts helped raise their standards. After much discussion he persuaded Doulton that both the pottery and the art school would benefit by working closely together. This resulted in a commission in 1864 for a series of terracotta heads depicting great potters to decorate a new extension to the factory. Sparkes was responsible for the design of this scheme and the modelling was carried out by one of his most talented young students, Percival Ball. At a later date this sculptor again worked with Doulton to produce two monumental figures for the Victoria and Albert Museum (cat. no. 23).

Assisting Ball on these projects was another young Lambeth student, George Tinworth. Sparkes induced Henry Doulton to employ Tinworth at the pottery as a modeller. One of his first architectural projects was to model several terracotta medallions based on antique coins. These featured in the architectural catalogue until the turn of the century. Similar examples can be seen on the former

STATUE OF SIR JOHN CROSBY,
BY SAMUEL NIXON

DOULTON & WATTS POTTERY,
LAMBETH, c. 1840

Albemarle Hotel (cat. no. 12). Doulton also began to expand their range of other architectural mouldings. Terracotta capitals, paterae, friezes and columns in a variety of styles were illustrated in their catalogues. This burst of activity at the pottery in the 1870s reflected the growing interest in terracotta detail for architectural purposes. Buildings were being erected at an unprecedented rate and the need for new, economical materials was growing.

The manufacturing process for terracotta components is quite complex. The architect's or manufacturer's drawings of the intended detail have first to be enlarged to allow for shrinkage of the material. From these drawings a plaster model is produced. A mould is then made from the model and clay is pressed into it to a thickness of approximately an inch. It is then reinforced by struts which cut the interior into chambers. The mould is then removed and the clay allowed to dry before being finished and fired. The main problems in the making of terracotta were encountered during the drying process as the block could distort considerably if not treated with care.

This necessarily slow process and the possibility of kiln disasters meant that delivery dates to the building sites were often erratic. This was the main objection raised against the material as its use became widespread; otherwise it fitted most of the requirements of the Victorian architect. It was more economical than stone, especially when repeated ornamental blocks were called for as these could be mass-produced. It was as strong as stone, although this was often disputed by its opponents despite frequent tests which proved its high crushing strength. It was more durable than stone, being better able to withstand the atmospheric corrosion in the new cities. Despite the material's obvious practical advantages, some architects discredited it on aesthetic grounds, maintaining that 'crockery cubes' were not a sufficiently dignified building material.

The architectural press did much to disperse these doubts, printing lengthy articles about the impressive historical pedigree of terracotta.

John Ruskin, the eminent art critic, was in favour of the material and helped raise its status by stressing the craftsmanship involved. 'A piece of terracotta,' he said 'which has been wrought by the human hand is worth all the stone in Carrara cut by machinery' (*Seven Lamps of Architecture, Lamp of Truth,* para. 20).

It was really the practical example set by the distinguished architects

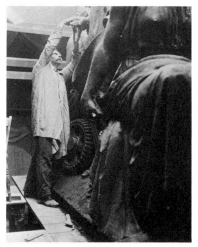

JOHN BROAD AT WORK ON TERRACOTTA GROUP FOR BRISBANE

Barry and Waterhouse which convinced others of terracotta's suitability for important public buildings. In 1868 Blashfield's terracotta was used by Charles Barry in the building of Dulwich College, regarded by many as one of the finest examples of modern terracotta. A few years later, Waterhouse, the greatest protagonist for the material, completed the Natural History Museum which demonstrated an excellent use of terracotta on a very large scale. It was one of Henry Doulton's early disappointments that he was not given the commission for

this major structure, although Waterhouse had visited his works. There was, however, a great deal of competition in the field of architectural ceramics. Firms like Blanchard and Blashfield had longer experience in the business and tended to get the early commissions. However, Doulton soon became one of the leading manufacturers and, from the late 1870s onwards, they supplied terracotta for many major buildings in a variety of styles by distinguished architects like Thomas Colcutt, Ernest George, Sir Aston Webb, Charles Fitzroy Doll and

TERRACOTTA DETAILS, MODELLED BY JOHN BROAD

many more. Waterhouse obviously overcame his earlier doubts about Doulton terracotta for he used it in his Refuge Assurance Buildings in Manchester (cat. no. 10).

The decorative styling of these public buildings was soon reflected in suburban architecture. Modest terrace houses would be embellished with a terracotta capital, paterae and perhaps an ornamental keystone over the window. More expensive houses would have more elaborate terracotta details like decorated window and doorheads, finials, friezes, and balu-

strades. The decorative effect on each property was often varied by arranging the same terracotta parts in a different order. These could be chosen from the architectural pattern books or made specially to the architect's specification. The terracotta business flourished rapidly and, by 1889, Henry Doulton had to open a new factory to supply the Midland towns. At Rowley Regis, near Birmingham, architectural terracotta, chimney pots and blue bricks began to be produced alongside the established drain pipe works. This new terracotta factory became the largest of its kind in the British Empire.

Much of Doulton's success can be attributed to the high standard of their architectural sculpture department. The resident artists designed all the architectural detail from a simple keystone to a frieze or tympanum. Many architects tended to rely on these artists' designs for their decorative features. It can be argued, therefore, that since ornament is the chief characteristic of Victorian architecture, Doulton artists should receive much of the credit for the appearance of the buildings they worked on. John Broad joined the Doulton Studios in 1873; a versatile and prolific sculptor, he executed many major terracotta commissions including the sculpture on the Great Central Hotel (cat. no. 20) and Harrods (cat. no. 3).

George Tinworth is undoubtedly the most famous terracotta sculptor of the Victorian era. The majority of his work was of a religious nature and his terracotta reliefs were incorporated in churches and chapels all over the world. He estimated that he had done more than 500 large-scale panels and even more smaller ones in his 47 years at the Lambeth studio. That was as well as his prolific output of art pottery, his occasional pulpits or fonts and his large-scale terracotta statues and fountains.

Doulton's resident artists, such as Broad, Tinworth and M V Marshall (cat. no. 36), produced the majority of their architectural terracotta but occasionally the firm worked with other freelance sculptors. One of the most ambitious sculptural projects at the Lambeth studio was instigated by John Bell, the distinguished Victorian sculptor. He suggested to Henry Doulton that a terracotta replica of the America Group on the Albert Memorial, which he had designed, would be an ideal centrepiece for the forthcoming Philadelphia Exhibition in 1876. Nothing on such a colossal scale had hitherto been produced in terracotta, but the venture was a complete success. At a later date John Broad worked on a similar heroic scale for a monument for Brisbane.

John Sparkes continued to introduce his artist friends and colleagues to Henry Doulton and they collaborated with him on several terracotta projects. Chief amongst these was W S Frith, a former pupil of Lambeth Art School who had become a teacher at the new City and Guilds School of Modelling founded by Sparkes in Kennington. Frith was an accomplished architectural and monumental sculptor. His projects with Doulton included a monumental fountain for the Glasgow Exhibition in 1888, which was one of the most impressive fountains made at Lambeth and involved the talents of several artists. A E Pearce, a Doulton designer, was responsible for the overall concept while the figure groups were modelled by John Broad, H Ellis, another Doulton sculptor, W S Frith and F W Pomeroy. The latter, also an ex-pupil of Lambeth School of Art, had become a sculptor of distinction (cat. no. 49).

As well as using sculpture as a decorative device, Victorian architects explored the decorative colour possibilities inherent in terracotta. The natural terracotta colours are buff and red, but many other colours can be made by mixing clays, introducing oxides or by dipping the blocks in coloured slip before firing. Buildings were erected with colour schemes ranging from pale buff and grey through various shades of orange and pink to dark maroon red. Buff terra-

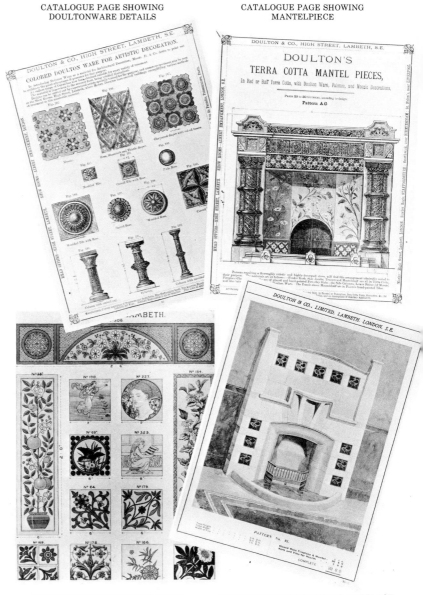

CATALOGUE PAGE SHOWING DOULTONWARE DETAILS

CATALOGUE PAGE SHOWING MANTELPIECE

CATALOGUE PAGE SHOWING TILES

CATALOGUE PAGE SHOWING FIREPLACE

cotta was often used in conjunction with brick or a contrasting shade of terracotta to produce a vivid striped effect. Contrasting shades of terracotta were effectively used on Doulton's own premises in 1876 (cat. no. 1a) which served as their architectural showpiece. An additional colour element was introduced by the use of tiles in salt-glazed stoneware.

Doultonware, as this material was called, was an adaptation of the body which Doulton had recently developed for their art pottery. In promoting this material for architectural purposes, Doulton believed that 'it will be welcomed by all who think the addition of colour advantageous to our buildings'. At this time there were many architects who felt that British buildings were drab and dowdy and they yearned for the gorgeousness of the East with its colourful tiled buildings. Ordinary earthenware tiles would not withstand the northern climate, and alternative coloured materials like polished granite and marbles were prohibitively expensive. Doultonware, having undergone a single firing to extremely high temperatures proved to be impervious to the action of damp, smoke and acid vapours and was thus welcomed as a substitute for other coloured materials.

Doultonware could be used either in the form of tiles or it could be modelled into bosses, balusters, columns and panels. Terracotta with jewel-like settings in Doultonware became a popular decorative combination, as used at St Paul's House, Leeds (cat. no. 9).

One of the earliest major schemes of salt-glazed stoneware decoration was the vestibule of Lloyds Bank (cat. no. 5). The medium has been fully exploited in this sumptuous interior. A new application of the material, Doultonware mosaic, was used in the dado whilst above this there are decorative areas in Silicon ware mosaic. This material, also adapted from an art pottery body, was as hard and vitreous as Doultonware but was unglazed and in quieter tints.

A more restrained use of Doultonware became the norm. Plain-coloured tiles were popular as a cladding material for the façades of public houses where a colourful, glittering exterior attracted the attention of prospective customers. The practical aspects of the material also recommend its extensive use. It was easily cleaned and therefore hygienic.

Doultonware also became a fashionable material for fountains and monuments. Many designs were produced by Arthur Pearce and also by the

TILE PANEL BY W J NEATBY IN HARROD'S MEAT HALL

architects Meredith and Pritchard, who were responsible for the most impressive surviving example, the Richard Eve Memorial at Kidderminster (cat. no. 54). It was also one of the few materials approved by the Metropolitan Drinking Fountains Association and they used it extensively for fountains and horse troughs in the London area.

Stoneware was recommended for both interior and exterior work on buildings, but Doulton also developed a range of glazed wares specially for interiors. Their first faience components were manufactured in 1873. The most popular finish was an opaque glazed terracotta in a wide range of majolica colours. The interior of the Rheemco building is an excellent example of this technique (cat. no. 63). To harmonise with their faience interiors, Doulton produced mantelpieces in a variety of different styles. The most elaborate designs made use of all the wares, terracotta, Doultonware, mosaic and tiles.

Doulton produced all types of tiling, including printed and hand-painted varieties. Some were individually decorated and often signed by one of the many faience department artists. Occasionally the studio undertook the decoration of major schemes like the interior of the Cecil Hotel which required thousand of tiles, all hand-painted in Indian designs (cat. no. 56).

Doulton had a very high reputation for the production of pictorial tile panels, also all hand-painted. Several artists specialised in this field, the most prolific being John Eyre, J H McLennan and Esther Lewis. Usually one artist was responsible for the design and another for the painting, but sometimes designer and painter were one. Tile pictures of all shapes and subject matter formed part of the interior decoration of pubs, banks, offices, shops, private houses and even public lavatories. The children's wards of hospitals also provided an admirable setting for Doulton tile murals. Plain tiling was extensively used for its hygienic qualities, but the addition of illustrated panels provided a source of entertainment for the young invalids. William Rowe and Margaret Thompson designed several series of nursery-rhyme panels which were used both in this country and abroad. Although the same subject is often repeated in different hospitals, the design and handling always varies slightly. However, as a guide to their production, Doulton published in 1904 a booklet *Pictures in Pottery* which illustrated many of these designs.

In 1885, Doulton introduced a new faience technique which abolished the

TILE PANEL BY J. EYRE AND J. McLENNAN

72

high-gloss effects of ordinary faience. Terracotta slabs were painted with a rich palette of colours which fired to a matt surface resembling fresco, hence the name for the ware, Vitreous Fresco. It was suitable for large figure compositions in public buildings, especially churches. A surviving example can be seen at St Luke's, Norwood.

The reflection of light on glazed exteriors was considered by many architects to be detrimental to the general effect of the building. By 1888, Doulton had also overcome this problem by developing a matt glazed stoneware. Called Carraraware, its white crystalline glaze made it similar in appearance to Carrara marble. Like Doultonware, this medium was first used for vases and small objects, but its suitability for architectural work was soon recognised. Carraraware is coated with enamel while still in an unfired state, then subjected to a single high firing. The resultant material is consequently as strong and as impervious to the atmosphere as Doultonware.

Carraraware was used on several significant buildings around the turn of the century. Architects of the Savoy Hotel and Debenhams, for instance, took advantage of its distinctive ivory finish which was much more subtle than the known alternative, white glazed bricks.

A large range of colours was gradually developed in Carraraware. The Birkbeck Bank was one of the earliest buildings to make use of the extended palette (cat. no. 4). With its colour scheme of deep blue-green, cinnamon brown and cream, it was one of the richest polychrome structures built in this country as well as being the largest example of a glazed ceramic building.

The most devoted protagonist for the use of coloured ceramics in architecture was the architect Halsey Ricardo. Throughout his career he continually extolled the practical qualities of glazed materials and stressed their decorative possibilities. His enthusiasm was shared by many

in the opening decades of the 20th century and several colourful Carraraware buildings were erected.

One of the more bizarre uses of Carraraware was the Everard Building in Bristol. W J Neatby, the designer, exploited the material's decorative possibilities to the full. The façade has been treated as a giant canvas with a pictorial decoration in vivid colours. When the structure was first unveiled there were traffic jams for a week as people gaped in astonishment. For the façades of other buildings Neatby modelled extensively in Carraraware, producing friezes, caryatids and masks in his distinctive Art Nouveau style. He also sculpted in plain terracotta, designed tile panels and entire interiors. This versatile artist was head of the architectural department at Doulton from 1890 to 1907 and during this time, apart from his prolific output, he considerably expanded the range of architectural ceramic techniques. He perfected a new process, Parian ware, which gave the same dull eggshell-like appearance in earthenware as Carrara did in stoneware. He used this for most of his interior schemes, sometimes with a raised outline effect, sometimes in intaglio. Examples can still be seen at Harrods and the Norwich Arcade (cat. nos. 3 & 77).

Another technique developed under Neatby's supervision was Polychrome Stoneware, inspired by the maiolica reliefs of the Italian Della Robbia school of sculptors. Again, it was found that the earthenware body used in Italy would not withstand the exposure to northern frost and rain. Doulton had previously achieved similar effects with their enamelled terracotta which is featured on St Bede's College, Manchester (cat. no. 7), but these reliefs still lacked the vibrancy of Della Robbia's work. After prolonged experimentation, however, they produced a stoneware equivalent. The body was first covered with a white slip which was allowed to dry. The colours were then painted on and the whole subjected to a salt firing to a temperature of 1250°. The

coloured coat fused perfectly with the body and was therefore capable of resisting the most testing atmospheric conditions, and the white ground had the effect of brightening the colour range and thus emulated the vivid palette of Della Robbia. Early panels in the material were used on a mission church in Glasgow in 1898, but the technique was not popular until after the First World War when it found favour with the sculptor Gilbert Bayes.

Neatby left Doulton in 1907 to work as a freelance designer. He still collaborated with them from time to time on special projects, and his influence was felt in the department until the war. Even his successor, the architect and sculptor Barry Pittar, worked in a style not dissimilar.

Inevitably, the war interrupted the output of Doulton's architectural studio and it was not until the 1920s that the demand for architectural ceramics was renewed. Carraraware proved itself to be adaptable to modern concepts of structure and design. Before the war, the first steel-framed structures had been effectively faced with the material and this continued in the inter-war years. Many of the new, reinforced concrete buildings were also clad in Carraraware as most architects did not want to leave the building in its naked state. The ivory-coloured glaze was most favoured for the new streamlined architecture and was extensively used on both modernist and classically inspired structures.

There was a general mistrust of the 'architectural frippery' of the Victorian and Edwardian periods and mouldings were cut to a minimum in the new designs. Surface pattern was achieved by varying the shapes and sizes of the Carraraware blocks or by putting emphasis on the joints. The 'lavatory convention' (a term coined at the time to describe unadventurous tiling) could also be avoided by exploiting the colour possibilities of the medium.

The twenties saw a renewed campaign 'to put a smile on the face of buildings' by using coloured faience. The RIBA held a colour competition in 1922 as an incentive to architects to apply permanent colour to buildings. Amongst the assessors was Halsey Ricardo who was again presenting the theories he first expounded at the beginning of the century. The £200 prize which was donated anonymously was won by Arthur Pearce from Doulton with a scheme in green, blue and white banded patterns. Harry Simeon, also a Doulton artist, received an honourable mention.

Coloured Carraraware became a popular medium for the facing of cinemas and other new entertainment centres. Apart from its endless decorative possibilities, it had practical advantages, like ease of cleaning, and also provided an ideal background for neon lighting.

Despite fierce competition from northern rivals, such as Leeds Fireclay or Hathern Ware, Doulton Carraraware was used on several interesting modernist designs. The most notable was the Sheen Cinema in Surrey (cat. no. 85). This was finished in bands of cream and green and was further enriched by two ceramic bas-reliefs of figures on horseback by Eric Aumonier; this sculptor often worked on architectural reliefs, his most celebrated being on the Temple of the Winds, above St James's Park underground.

Several other sculptors collaborated with Doulton on architectural projects. Frank Dobson designed an original series of semi-abstract panels in gold stoneware for the Hays Wharf building (cat. no. 91).

Dobson was the most avant-garde sculptor to work with Doulton. Others tended to be more traditional like George Edward Kruger-Gray. His work for Doulton included a Polychrome Stoneware relief depicting a king which was used as an advertising plaque for Greene King Breweries.

Gilbert Bayes had the longest and most prolific association with Doulton. This very talented artist had

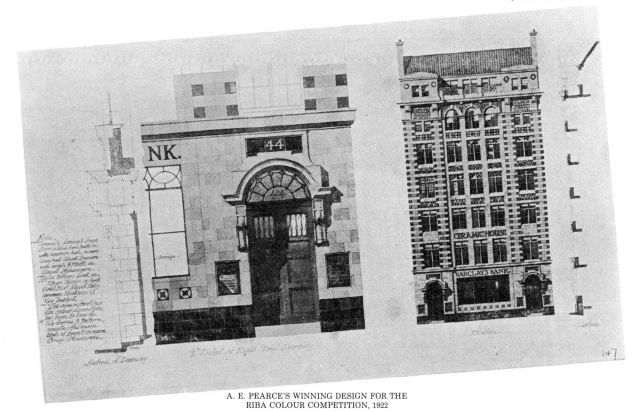

A. E. PEARCE'S WINNING DESIGN FOR THE
RIBA COLOUR COMPETITION, 1922

a considerable reputation as an architectural sculptor and also exhibited regularly at the Royal Academy. He worked in a variety of media, but particularly favoured coloured materials. It was this interest which prompted his work with the Doulton pottery. Polychrome Stoneware proved to be an ideal medium for his sculpture, being resilient enough for outdoor locations. His first essays in the material were a fountain which he exhibited at Wembley in 1924 and a roundel influenced by Della Robbia. This was followed by several panels, mostly inspired by romantic subject matter and executed in his characteristic style, mixing realistic and formal elements. Most of these were used on buildings by Cowles Voysey and Ian Hamilton who both shared his views on introducing colourful details to improve the environment. Hamilton had particularly strong ideas on this subject and was responsible for many innovations which improved the quality of life at the St Pancras Housing Association's estates. Bayes' sculpture also greatly enriched the complex (cat. no. 88).

The most ambitious decorative scheme ever executed in Polychrome Stoneware was Bayes' 50-foot frieze depicting 'Pottery Through the Ages' which dominated the façade of Doulton House. It was completed in 1939 and is close in style to Bayes' early work in artificial stone on the Saville Theatre. Doulton House was one of the last buildings to be faced with their ceramics. War again put a stop to the activities of the architectural department and it did not revive afterwards. In the post-war years, austerity and changes in fashion meant that there was no longer any demand for ceramic sculpture or architectural materials. Moreover, many architects now paid lip service to the 'structural honesty' concept and so deliberately avoided facing their concrete buildings with ceramics or any other materials. The Lambeth factory finally closed in 1956, thus ending Doultons' interest in architectural ceramics.

DOULTON HOUSE FRIEZE BY
GILBERT BAYES

MAJOR MIXED MEDIA STRUCTURES

1a FORMER DOULTON SHOWROOMS & STUDIOS
Corner of Lambeth High St &
Black Prince Rd, London SE1
Date: 1876–8
Architects: Tarring Son & Wilkinson
Illustration: *Building News,* 1876,
Vol. XXXI, p. 468

This ornate, Gothic-style structure
was built as a permanent advertisement for Doulton architectural
ceramics. It is profusely decorated
with red and buff terracotta details
and with Doultonware bosses,
plaques, lintels and sills. Above the
doorway is a tympanum modelled in
terracotta by G Tinworth, depicting
Henry Doulton in the Lambeth studio
with some of his artists. This building
is all that remains of the extensive
range of Doulton terracotta
structures that used to dominate the
Lambeth embankment. Towering
above them was a chimney 233 feet
high, modelled as an Italian
campanile, supposedly on the advice
of John Ruskin.

1b DOULTON HOUSE (DESTROYED)
Albert Embankment, London SE1
Date: 1939
Architect: T P Bennett
Sculptor: G Bayes
Illustration: *Pottery and Glass,* 1950,
Mar., pp. 48–9

Demolished in 1978, Doulton House
was originally the headquarters of
Doulton & Co. This modernist building was entirely faced with ivory and
black Carraraware. The most striking
feature was the entrance, flanked by
four fluted pilasters of gold Carraraware, and surmounted by a 50 feet
relief panel in coloured stoneware by
Gilbert Bayes depicting 'Pottery
through the Ages'. A smaller Bayes
panel on the side of the building
showed Dutch potters arriving in
Lambeth in the 17th century. Both
panels were saved from destruction

1a FORMER DOULTON PREMISES,
ALBERT EMBANKMENT

1a ARCHITECT'S DRAWING

1b ARCHITECT'S DRAWING

and are now being restored. The large panel will be re-erected in Lambeth.

In the entrance hall were tile panels depicting the coats of arms of towns and cities in which Doulton had factories and offices, and elsewhere in the building were other examples of Doulton ceramics, including a view indicator on the roof.

2 WOOLPITS
Peaslake Rd, Ewhurst, Surrey
(now a private school)
Date: 1885–8
Architect: E George & Peto
Artists: G Tinworth, A E Pearce,
J Eyre
Illustration: *British Architect*, 1888,
Vol. XXIX, pp. 20, 60

Sir Henry Doulton took advantage of the skills of many of his artists when building his country house. However, most of the decorative ceramic features have not survived. These included a splendid billiard room in faience designed by Pearce, a series of Shakespearian panels painted by Eyre and a Tinworth terracotta panel, Abraham and the Angel, which surmounted the entrance. The buff terracotta details and the rest of the exterior still retain their original character.

3 HARRODS
Brompton Rd, London SW1
Dates: 1901, 1911 and in 1930–4
Architects: C W Stephens; L D Blanc
(1930–4 extension)
Sculptor: J Broad
Tile designer: W J Neatby
Illustrations: *Victorian Ceramic Tiles*,
J Barnard, pl. 109; *Architect and
Building News*, 1971, Sep., p. 48

This familiar Knightsbridge landmark was a major Doulton commission. It was built in three stages: the 1901 façade and the 1911 side elevation were constructed in a warm pink terracotta with French Renaissance details. The extension at the rear was built in the 1930s in the then unfashionable unglazed brown terracotta to match the rest. Some coloured stoneware, including a new

1b SMALL PANEL FROM NORTH ELEVATION, BEFORE COLOURING

3 BASIL STREET ELEVATION

bronze finish was also incorporated in the design. Inside, the meat hall is decorated with Parian ware tiling designed by Neatby in his distinctive Art Nouveau style; the scheme consists of 20 medallions depicting farming and hunting scenes, set in an overall pattern of stylised fishes, birds and trees.

4 BIRKBECK BANK (DESTROYED)

Chancery Lane, London WC2
Date: 1895–6
Architect: T E Knightley
Sculptor: J Broad
Tile designer/painter: J H McLennan
Illustrations: *Architect and Building News*, 1948, Vol. CVCIV, pp. 466–7; *Architectural Review*, 1965, Vol. CXXXVIII, pp. 338–41

This High Victorian ceramic extravaganza was destroyed in 1965. The exterior was decorated with polychrome Carraraware, in bright green, biscuit and brown, with an abundance of sculptural details in a general Renaissance style. Flanking the entrance were terracotta groups representing Commerce and Britannia, and applied to the building were a series of portrait busts of famous artists and scientists. Inside, arranged around the domed banking hall were 16 semi-circular tile panels representing trades, industries and scenes connected with banking. Most of the offices were additionally lined with faience, and the centrepiece of the boardroom was a glazed ware fireplace.

5 LLOYDS BANK (ORIGINALLY THE PALSGROVE HOTEL)

Fleet St, London EC4
Date: 1883
Architect: G Cuthbert
Tile designer/painter: J H McLennan
Illustration: *Victorian Ceramic Tiles*, J Barnard, pl. 115

The impressive entrance in coloured Doultonware and Silicon ware mosaic is a dramatic mixture of Baroque and Islamic details. The adjoining corridor is set with tiling with putti

and swag motifs and an heraldic panel. In the banking area there are several tile pictures painted with scenes from Ben Jonson plays. There are also many floral panels.

6 IMPERIAL HOTEL (DESTROYED)

Russell Sq, London WC1
Dates: 1907 & 1911
Architect: C Fitzroy Doll
Sculptors: J Broad, W J Neatby & others
Illustration: *Architectural Review*, 1966, Vol. CXL, pp. 451–4

This extravagent red brick structure was profusely ornamented with buff terracotta motifs in Jacobean, Spanish and Germanic styles. They included gargoyles, heraldic panels and life-size statues of Edward VII, Queen Alexandria, Caesar and Charlemagne. The main tower was flanked with a series of terracotta maidens, very similar to the set of muses used by Doll for the public house 'Apollo and the Muses' (see 19 below). Inside, the Winter Gardens and the Turkish Bath were tiled with cream faience, with decorative details mostly by Neatby. Several of the sculptures still survive in the courtyard of the new building.

7 ST BEDE'S COLLEGE

Alexandra Rd, Manchester
Date: 1878–84
Architects: Dunn & Hanson
Sculptor: J Broad

This red terracotta building, in the style of a Florentine palazzo, has several unusual decorative features. The main entrance is flanked by four vitreous enamelled terracotta panels modelled in high relief by Broad which represent the academic disciplines; these are the only known example of this particular ceramic technique. Crawling on the wall above are a number of giant terracotta bees, while another amusing detail are the series of modelled heads which peer down from the window pediments; Queen Victoria looks particularly uncomfortable.

4 PANEL OF GEORGE STEPHENSON, UNGLAZED STATE

6 IMPERIAL HOTEL

4 INTERIOR VIEW

6 FAIENCE DOORWAY

5 MAIN ENTRANCE

HUMOUR. 1598

A Most perfect Toledo I assure you sir

Cap^tn Bobadil

You talk of Morgaly, Excalibur, Durindana or so!

5 TILE PANEL IN BANKING AREA

8 NEW PALACE THEATRE

Union St, Plymouth, Devon
Date: 1898
Architects: Wimperis & Arber
Sculptor: W J Neatby
Illustration: *British Architect*, 1898,
Nov., p. 382

This richly-decorated structure in a
variety of materials has been marred
by the addition of a modern fascia.
The ground floor is in brown glazed
ware, while the upper part of the
façade is in varied tones of brown and
buff terracotta. Set into this are two
large semi-circular panels in vitreous
enamels, depicting scenes from the
Spanish Armada, adapted from paintings by Sir Oswald Brierly. Many
other decorative details have a
nautical flavour, including the friezes
of ships with billowing sails, and
several mermaids.

9 ST PAUL'S HOUSE

St Paul's St, Leeds
Date: 1878
Architect: T Ambler
Illustration: *High Victorian Design*,
S Jervis, p. 244

An impressive Victorian warehouse
built of red brick and buff terracotta
in a Moorish Venetian style, the
building is characterised by its
minarets and by the doorway
decorated with Doultonware tiles in
vivid blue and white. The structure
has recently been fully restored.

10 REFUGE ASSURANCE BUILDINGS

Oxford Rd, Manchester
Date: 1891–1912
Architect: A Waterhouse & Sons

A variety of Doulton architectural
wares was employed on this building.
The Renaissance-style detailing on
the façades is in dark red terracotta,
while the main entrance courtyard is
in buff glazed terracotta. Another
entrance has a vestibule tiled in a
dramatic mixture of Islamic and
Renaissance styles; the interior is
richly decorated with faience in
shades of cream and green.

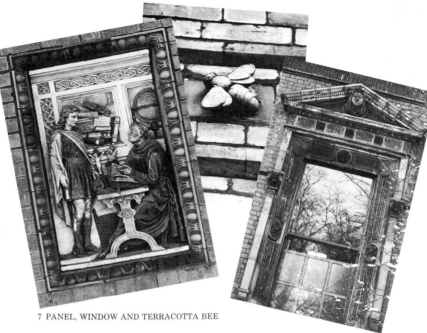

7 PANEL, WINDOW AND TERRACOTTA BEE

8 DRAWING BY RAFFLES DAVISON

10 REFUGE ASSURANCE BUILDINGS

TERRACOTTA BUILDINGS

11 FORMER STANFORD'S PREMISES
26–27 Cockspur St, London SW1
Date: c. 1888
Architect: W B Williams

Originally the premises of Stanford's, the map specialists, this red brick and terracotta building is suitably decorated with panels above the fascia depicting Atlas and other geographical motifs. The ground floor has recently been modernised, and the whole building cleaned.

12 FORMER ALBEMARLE HOTEL
Corner of Albemarle St and Piccadilly, London W1
Date: 1888
Architects: E George & Peto
Illustration: *British Architect*, 1893, Dec., p. 436

A pinkish red terracotta building with Renaissance-style decorative details. The large medallions set into the window bays are similar to those illustrated in Doulton architectural catalogues, many of which are designed for series production by G Tinworth. They were based on coins in the British Museum.

13 PALACE THEATRE
Shaftesbury Ave, London W1
Date: 1890
Architect: T E Colcutt
Sculptor: W Smith

Built in Collcutt's northern Renaissance style with some Spanish details, this theatre has suffered by having its dramatic concave façade largely obscured by hoardings and neon lighting. However, the side elevations show clearly the interesting contrast between plain brickwork and the finely detailed friezes in pink terracotta.
    Another London theatre with Doulton terracotta is the Royal Court, Sloane Sq.

14 FRENCH PROTESTANT CHURCH
8, 9 Soho Sq, London W1
Date: 1891
Architect: Sir Aston Webb
Illustration: *Builder*, 1893, Vol. LXIV, p. 448

A rare surviving example of a church decorated inside and out with Doulton terracotta. The inside walls are decorated with buff and light brown terracotta creating an interesting striped effect. The gallery and pulpit are in buff and are decorated with a mixture of Renaissance and Gothic motifs. The exterior façade is in red brick and deep red terracotta.

15 FORMER REDFERN GALLERY
26, 27 Conduit St, London W1
Date: 1896
Architect: A H Kersey
Sculptors: W J Neatby & G Elmes
Illustration: *British Architect*, 1896, Vol. XLVI, pp. 129–30

Only the upper storeys which include decorative panels survive, which is unfortunate as the ground-floor entrance was clearly the best feature of this building. It was a hooded porch decorated with coffered panels, foliate scrolls and masks. A pair of caryatids, vigorously modelled by Elmes, at one time flanked the doorway, but were later removed as some clients considered them indecent.

16 SHOPS AND OFFICES
40 & 42–6 Wigmore St, London W1
Date: 40, 1890; 42–6, 1883
Architects: 40, T E Colcutt; 42–46, E George & Peto
Illustration: 40, *Builder*, 1890, Vol. LVIII, p. 376

These adjoining buildings by eminent architects show the contrasting effects achieved with terracotta. 40, in red terracotta, has unfortunately lost the original ground floor with its hooded entrances and sculptural details, but 42–6 with its buff terracotta and red brick is a good example of the vivid polychrome effects popular at the time.

17 SHOPS AND HOUSES
104–8 & 125–9 Mount St, London W1
Date: 1886
Architects: 104–8, E George & Peto; 125–9 W H Powell

Mount Street includes an interesting variety of terracotta effects, by a number of different manufacturers. Doulton were responsible for these two ranges. The former, the first building on the Grosvenor Estate to be entirely faced with terracotta, is in a French Flamboyant Gothic style, while the latter is in the Queen Anne style. Here, buff terracotta is alternated with bands of red brick, to produce the then popular 'streaky bacon' effect.

18 RUSSELL HOTEL
Russell Sq, London WC1
Date: 1898
Architect: C Fitzroy Doll
Sculptor: H C Fehr

This vast red terracotta structure, built in a general French Renaissance style with baronial details, is now rather isolated in the formal surroundings of Russell Square, having lost its erstwhile mate, the Imperial Hotel. There are many splendid details, however, including the four sculptures by Fehr of England's great Queens, the portrait busts on the side elevation and the columns decorated with dancing cherubs.

19 APOLLO AND THE MUSES PUBLIC HOUSE (DESTROYED)
Tottenham Court Road, London W1
Date: 1898
Architect: C Fitzroy Doll
Sculptor: J Broad

Another Doll extravaganza, this pub, demolished in 1961, was decorated with over life-size statues of Apollo and the Muses modelled by Broad in buff terracotta. Many of the figures survive in private collections, including the example in this exhibition. Another can be seen in St George's Gardens, Heathcote Street, London WCI. This one was presented to the

Mayor of St Pancras and put on public display after removal from the pub.

20 BRITISH RAIL HEADQUARTERS (FORMERLY GREAT CENTRAL HOTEL)
222 Marylebone Rd, London NW1
Date: 1897–9
Architect: Colonel R W Edis
Sculptor: J Broad

A large red brick structure with buff terracotta dressings, mostly Renaissance in style. The main features are the two female figures in the spandrels of the doorway, representing Night and Day.

21 ORCHARD HOUSE
Abbey Orchard St, London W1
Date: c. 1900
Sculptor: W J Neatby
Illustration: *Studio*, 1903, Vol. 29, pp. 114–5

Two buff terracotta panels modelled in low relief in an Art Nouveau style by Neatby are set above the doorways. One features a stylised tree with ornamental lettering, the other two peacocks. Both are badly in need of cleaning.

22 TOWN HOUSE
52 Cadogan Sq, London SW1
Date: 1886
Architects: E George & Peto
Illustration: *Builder*, 1886, Vol. L, p. 708

This highly decorative and unusual red brick house has elaborate buff terracotta dressings with a wealth of Flemish and Mannerist detail. The group of terracotta figures situated at the top of the main window bay is particularly effective, especially the jester playing a violin.

23 VICTORIA & ALBERT MUSEUM, QUADRANGLE
Brompton Rd, London SW7
Date: 1862–1901
Architects: Captain Fowke; Sir Aston Webb
Sculptor: P Ball

The museum quadrangle, which was

18 QUEEN FIGURE

19 THE MUSE, *EUTERPE*, IN ST GEORGE'S GARDENS

20 SPANDREL DEPICTING NIGHT, BEFORE INSTALLATION

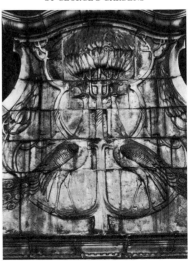

21 DOORWAY DETAIL

built in stages, is faced with terra-cotta supplied by different manufac-turers. Doulton, in conjunction with Percival Ball, produced the terracotta groups of 'Instruction' which terminate the balustrade on the north side. In 1901 they supplied the terra-cotta for the eastern side which was designed to match the earlier façade opposite.

24 FORMER POST OFFICE (NOW DEPARTMENT OF EMPLOYMENT)
67 Upper Tooting Rd, London SW17
Date: c. 1890
Architects: HM's Offices of Works

This compact little building shows how well brick and terracotta could be used on a small scale. Decorative features include low relief foliate scrollwork and other Renaissance details, and a heraldic panel with lion and unicorn in high relief above the doorway. The nearby Tooting Library, at 75 Mitcham Rd, is another Doulton terracotta structure, designed by W Hunt.

25 ST PANCRAS BATHS
Prince of Wales Rd, London NW5
Date: 1900
Architect: T W Aldwinckle
Sculptor: W S Frith (stylistic attribution)

This red brick bath house has impres-sive buff terracotta sculpture; the Men's First and Second Class entrances are richly decorated with personifications of river gods and goddesses, including Father Thames, while vigorous statues of St Pancras and St George stand in niches below the gable.

26 SHOPS AND OFFICES
54–5 Cornhill, London EC3
Date: 1893
Architect: E Runtz
Sculptor: W J Neatby
Illustration: *Artist*, 1899, Vol. XXV, p. 94

This pinkish red terracotta building is ornamented with sculptural details by Neatby. Particularly interesting

22 CADOGAN SQUARE

25 FIGURE OF ST PANCRAS

are the elaborate fascia, and the grotesque devils which peer down at the street from the gables. Similar grotesque creatures were used on St Pancras Baths (see 25 above).

27 EAST HAM LIBRARY, TOWN HALL AND INSTITUTE
Barking Rd, High St South, London
Date: 1903 (completed)
Architects: Library, A H Campbell; Town Hall and Institute, H Cheers

This extensive complex is all in dark red brick and light red terracotta. The structure is dominated by a clock tower with an open belfry and pinnacles. Beneath the clock are decorative heads in Art Nouveau style. Most of the porches and door-ways have elaborate Renaissance details.

28 GENERAL HOSPITAL
Steelhouse Lane, Birmingham
Date: 1892–7
Architect: W Henman
Sculptor: J W Rollins
Illustration: *British Architect*, 1897, Jul., pp. 488–99

Although the main complex of dark red terracotta buildings remain, they have been stripped of most of the major decorative features. Originally, the entrance to the Administrative Block was enriched by a group of three female figures symbolising Medicine, Surgery and Philanthropy holding up the Lamb of Life and tread-ing under their feet the Serpent of Death. At the patients' entrance were three other monumental figures representing Air, Purity and Light. In the courtyard there was a large fountain presented by Sir Henry Doulton.

29 QUEEN'S COLLEGE
Paradise St, Birmingham
Date: 1843, remodelled c. 1890
Architects: Drury & Bateman; remodelling, Mansell & Mansell.

The refaced front of this building is in a mixture of Tudor and Gothic styles, with sculpted monsters and grotesques, pierced tracery and fan vaulting, all in buff terracotta. Above the entrance is an impressive group of Queen Victoria flanked by a lion and unicorn.

30 CITY ARCADES
Union St, Birmingham
Dates: 1898; 1901
Architects: Newton & Cheadle
Sculptor: W J Neatby
Illustrations: *Studio*, 1903, Vol. 29, p. 116; *Artist*, 1900, Vol. XXVIII, p. 107

Constructed in red brick and terracotta, this shopping arcade is greatly enlivened by Neatby's decorative details which include terminal piper figures, a frieze of fantastic beasts and cartouches containing stylised heads. Inside is a blue and green faience balustrade formed by entwined beasts and scrollwork.

31 LIBRARY
Garrick St, Snow Hill, Wolverhampton
Date: 1900–2
Architect: H T Hare
Illustration: *Edwardian Architecture*, A Service, p. 106

Although predominantly a red brick building, buff terracotta details create an interesting striped effect on the façade and around the windows. Other terracotta features include the cupolas and panels carrying the names of famous writers.

32 CITY WHOLESALE MARKET (DESTROYED)
Halford St, Leicester
Date: 1900
Architect: W Brand
Sculptor: W J Neatby

The market entrance was originally surrounded by a low relief terracotta panel enriched with mermaids and fishes in Art Nouveau style; the fish motif was continued in the voussoirs. This design is very similar to the mermaid panels on the Palace Theatre, Plymouth (see 8). This panel was preserved when the market was demolished, and will eventually be re-erected as a decorative feature on a new development.

27 DETAIL OF THE TOWER AT EAST HAM LIBRARY, TOWN HALL AND INSTITUTE

28 VIEW OF GENERAL HOSPITAL COURTYARD, DURING ROYAL VISIT

32 MARKET ENTRANCE

33 SCHOOL OF ART EXTENSION
Grosvenor Sq, Manchester
Date: 1897
Architect: J Gibbons Sankey
Sculptor: W J Neatby
Illustration: *Artist*, 1899, Vol. XXV,
pp. 95, 99

This unassuming red brick extension
to the earlier structure has pinkish
terracotta dressings in a general Art
Nouveau style. The spandrels are
decorated with angels holding shields,
and there is a commemorative panel
in stylish script.

**34 FORMER BOARD SCHOOL
(NOW SALFORD EDUCATION
DEPARTMENT)**
Chapel Street, Salford,
Greater Manchester
Date: 1894
Architects: Woodhouse & Willoughby
Sculptor: W J Neatby
Illustration: *British Architect*, 1896,
Vol. XLVI, p. 205

A light red terracotta building in the
English Renaissance style with
several decorative panels of scrollwork and masks in Neatby's distinctive style.

**35 FORMER COMMERCIAL
CHAMBERS (NOW WALLPAPER
HOUSE)**
Red Lion St, Norwich, Norfolk
Date: 1901–3
Architect: G Skipper
Illustration: *Building News*, 1904,
Vol. LXXXVI, pp. 233–5

These offices in cream and dark brown
terracotta were originally designed
for an accountant, Charles Larking,
by one of Norwich's best-known late
Victorian architects. The building is
personalised by cartouches carrying
Larking's initials, while seated in the
gable is a large figure engrossed in
writing – designed presumably to
inspire the accountants within. Great
care was taken to harmonise the
colour and finish of the terracotta
with the adjoining stone building;
now, after over-zealous cleaning, the
texture is even more stone like.

Skipper also used Doulton terra-
cotta details for the nearby
Haymarket Chambers, in the
Haymarket, now a clothes shop
(Snob Ltd).

**36 CANADIAN PACIFIC
RAILROAD HOTEL**
Vancouver, Canada
Date: c. 1913
Architect: F Swales

During the Edwardian period
Doulton carried out several important
terracotta commissions in Canada,
the completed components being
shipped from the factory for assembly
on site. The decoration was often
more extravagent than contemporary
work in England, a feature well illustrated by this hotel with its whimsical
heads of bison and moose.

Another example is the offices for
the *Calgary Herald*, built in 1913,
richly ornamented with caricatures of
newspaper staff modelled by Mark
Marshall. Other Canadian buildings
include St John's Church, Saskatoon,
built in 1913 and decorated with
bizarre bird and fish details probably
also by Marshall, the King George
Hotel, Saskatoon, and the Canada
Life Assurance Building, Calgary.
Doulton terracotta was also used in
Mexico, South Africa, India, Natal
and many other countries.

TERRACOTTA STATUARY, FOUNTAINS AND MONUMENTAL WORK

---

37 FOUNTAIN
Kennington Park,
Kennington Park Rd, London SE11
Date: 1869
Designer: J Sparkes
Sculptor: G Tinworth

This buff terracotta fountain was
donated by Sir Henry Doulton. Only
the central shaft remains today, but
this includes an early sculpture by
Tinworth, the 'Pilgrimage of Life'.

36 CARICATURES FOR CALGARY HERALD
BUILDING

38 FAWCETT STATUE (DESTROYED)

Vauxhall Park, London SW8
Date: 1893
Sculptor: G Tinworth

This buff terracotta monument to
Henry Fawcett, the blind statesman,
was presented to the park by Sir
Henry Doulton. It was removed in
1960. The figures were arranged on a
tall plinth decorated with relief panels
illustrating Fawcett's life and work.
A maquette of the statue was shown
at the Chicago Exhibition in 1893.

Tinworth also modelled life-size
statues of C Bradlaugh, MP for
Northampton, which still stands in
Abington Sq, Northampton (although
now painted white) and C H Spurgeon,
the Calvinist preacher; this stood
originally at Stockwell Orphanage,
but has subsequently been split up,
and two panels resited at Spurgeon's
College, South Norwood Hill, and
Spurgeon's Homes, Birchington,
Kent. Relief portraits by Tinworth of
other Victorian worthies included
Lord Shaftesbury, Samuel Morley,
Passmore Edwards and Cameron
(see 50).

39 LUNETTES AT THE GUARDS CHAPELS (DESTROYED)

Birdcage Walk, London SW1
Date: 1878
Architect: G E Street
Sculptor: G Tinworth

After submitting a panel of David &
Goliath to Street, Tinworth was
commissioned to produce twenty-eight
semi-circular reliefs for the chapel.
The subjects were taken from both
Old and New Testaments, and the
series began with Adam and Eve and
finished with the Parables. Most of
the lunettes were destroyed when the
Chapel was bombed, but some survive
in private hands. A complete set of
maquettes in saltglazed stoneware
also survive.

40 REREDOS & PANELS, ST MARY'S CHURCH

Lambeth Rd, London SW1
Date: 1888–9

36 DETAILS FROM CPR HOTEL

38 PANEL SHOWING SAMUEL MORLEY
(DESTROYED)

38 TINWORTH AT WORK ON THE
FAWCETT MAQUETTE

39 MAQUETTE DEPICTING
DAVID & GOLIATH

Designer: J Oldrid Scott
Sculptor: G Tinworth

This reredos in buff terracotta with
Doultonware columns was erected by
Sir Henry Doulton in memory of his
wife. It was badly damaged during the
war, and now only the central Crucifixion panel remains. It was originally
flanked by arched bays containing
figures of Moses, Elijah, Peter and
Paul, and wings with quatrefoil
portrait panels of archbishops. There
are two other Tinworth memorial
panels in the church, Christ Blessing
the Children, 1888, and Christ in the
Temple as a Boy, 1899.
   Other London churches decorated
by Tinworth panels included St Mary
Magdalene, Trinity Road, SW17,
St Thomas's Hospital Chapel,
Lambeth Palace Rd, SE1, Baptist
Church House, Southampton Row,
WC1, and St Augustine with
St Philip, Newark St, E1.

41 PANEL AT ST ANNE'S CHURCH

St Anne's Crescent, London SW18
Date: 1896
Sculptor: J Broad

Set into the apse is a panel depicting
The Last Supper, based on the
Leonardo fresco. It is modelled in buff
terracotta with a painted blue background. Originally shown at the
Royal Academy in 1896, the panel was
built into the church two years later.

42 REREDOS AT ST JOHN'S CHURCH

Landsdowne Crescent, London W11
Date: c. 1890
Designer: Sir Aston Webb
Sculptor: E Halse

This elaborate terracotta reredos in
Perpendicular Gothic style has been
insensitively painted over.
   The panels depicting the life of
St John were acclaimed as the
principal work of Emeline Halse, a
sculptress who exhibited frequently
at the Royal Academy.

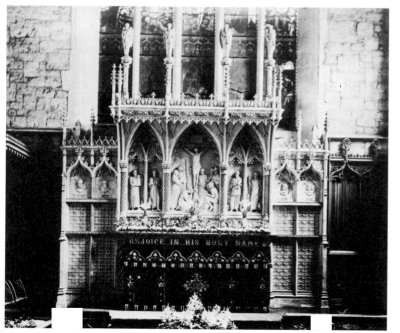

REJOICE IN HIS HOLY NAME

40 REREDOS IN ITS ORIGINAL CONDITION

43 SIR HENRY DOULTON'S MAUSOLEUM

South Metropolitan Cemetery,
Norwood High St, London SE27
Date: 1897

This surprisingly simple and
unassuming structure in red brick
and deep pink terracotta has gables
containing low relief sculptural
panels. The designer has not been
recorded.

Also in this cemetery is Henry
Tate's memorial chapel, designed by
E George and Peto, and decorated
with Doulton terracotta.

Another terracotta memorial, the
Stearne Mausoleum, can be seen at
Nunhead Cemetery, Linden Grove,
SE15; this is unusually decorated
with Celtic motifs.

44 REREDOS, YORK MINSTER

St Stephen's Chapel, York
Date: 1876
Designer: G E Street
Sculptor: G Tinworth
Illustration: *Country Life*, 1960, Sep.,
pp. 431, 633

The reredos was originally an
elaborate Gothic-style carved oak
triptych, but the wings were removed
after being damaged, leaving only the
central panel. This includes
Tinworth's large terracotta relief
panel, The First Hour of the Crucifixion. This splendid panel, in a grey
terracotta richly decorated with
gilding, is packed with figures
modelled in high relief.

45 PANELS, BROMLEY-DAVENPORT CHAPEL

Capesthorne, nr Macclesfield,
Cheshire
Date: 1887
Sculptor: G Tinworth
Illustrations: *British Architect*, 1886,
Vol. XXVI, p. 6; *Black and White*,
1898, Feb., p. 183

Four low relief panels are arranged
between the windows on the north
and south walls. The subjects are
Temptation and Faith, and Darkness
and Light, symbolised by Adam and
Eve in the Garden and the Uplifting

of the Serpent in the Wilderness, and
the Crucifixion and the Ascension.

Panels by Tinworth were installed
in churches and chapels throughout
Britain and abroad.

46 SCULPTURE, WHITWORTH PARK (DESTROYED)

Oxford Rd, Manchester
Date: c. 1875
Sculptor: G Tinworth

Only the base remains of this terracotta group which depicted Christ
Blessing the Little Children. According to Tinworth, this was one of his
favourite subjects.

47 ENGLISH CHURCH OF ST ALBAN

Copenhagen
Date: 1887
Architect: A W Blomfield
Sculptor: G Tinworth

Tinworth produced a reredos, pulpit
and font for this church, all in an
Early English Gothic style. The
reredos, a triptych in pink terracotta,
included panels representing The
Betrayal, The Lord Appearing to
Thomas and Going Home. The pulpit
and font were both in a combination
of terracotta and Doultonware.

A number of other church fixtures
were made by Doulton, including a
pulpit and font shown at Philadelphia
in 1876, and a pulpit at the East Sheen
Congregational Church, Mortlake.

48 MEMORIAL TO QUEEN VICTORIA

Victoria Park, Newbury, Berkshire
Date: c. 1901
Sculptor: J Broad

The red terracotta statue of the
standing Queen is flanked by two
large reclining lions. Broad modelled
several large-scale statues of Queen
Victoria, as well as a small seated
version. One example used to stand on
the Embankment in front of the old
Doulton works. Broad also modelled
large-scale statues of Edward VII and
Queen Alexandra.

Another Broad statue is that of

45 TEMPTATION PANEL

46 SCULPTURE IN ITS ORIGINAL
CONDITION

48 QUEEN VICTORIA, FORMERLY ON
ALBERT EMBANKMENT

General Gordon, which still stands in
the park at Gravesend, Kent.

49 VICTORIA FOUNTAIN
Glasgow Green, Glasgow
Date: 1887
Designers: A E Pearce & W S Frith
Sculptors: W S Frith, F Pomeroy,
J Broad, H Ellis
Illustration: *British Architect*, 1888,
Vol. XXX, p. 456

This spectacular memorial fountain
in red terracotta stands 46 feet high.
Designed in a French Renaissance
style, it was made for the Glasgow
International Exhibition of 1888. The
sculptural scheme illustrates the
Empire, with over life-size figurative
groups symbolising Canada
(by W S Frith), Australia (by
F W Pomeroy), South Africa
(by H Ellis) and India (by J Broad).
The crowning figure of Queen
Victoria was modelled by W S Frith.
  The whole structure is sadly
decayed and is in need of restoration.

50 SIR CHARLES CAMERON
FOUNTAIN & CLOCKTOWER
Woodside Crescent, Glasgow
Date: 1896
Sculptor: G Tinworth
Illustration: *British Architect*, 1896,
Vol. XLV, p. 201

An octagonal monument in the French
Renaissance style, whose base and
basin are in Peterhead granite, and its
upper section in red terracotta. The
fountain was dedicated to Sir Charles
Cameron, a Glasgow physician
responsible for many social and
medical reforms; a bronze portrait
plaque of him, modelled by Tinworth,
is set into the structure.

BUILDINGS AND OTHER
STRUCTURES WITH
DOULTONWARE DECORATION

51 OFFICES
17, 18 Henrietta St, London WC2
Date: c. 1900
Architect: J T Woodard

This building, with its upper storeys

47 PULPIT EXHIBITED AT THE
PHILADELPHIA CENTENNIAL, 1876

49 VICTORIA FOUNTAIN

49 CANADA GROUP,
BEFORE INSTALLATION

in red brick, and its ground floor faced with blue and green Doultonware, has recently been cleaned showing how effective this combination of materials can be. The façade is decorated with moulded foliate panels.

Nearby, at 36 Southampton Street, is another building faced with this material. This is more extensive and varied in style, but has suffered from subsequent alteration. However, this is a rare example that actually carries Doulton factory marks.

52 ROYAL HOSPITAL FOR CHILDREN & WOMEN
Waterloo Rd, London SE1
Date: 1903–5
Architects: Waring & Nicholson
Illustration: *Building News*, 1903, Vol. LXXXV, pp. 67–9

This impressive red brick and brown terracotta building has elaborate Doultonware ornamentation in an Art Nouveau style. The entrance porch, in green Doultonware, was donated by H Lewis Doulton; the balconies are decorated with ornate lettering in the same material. The whole structure is badly in need of care and attention, and so its extremely colourful appearance is hard to determine at the moment.

The Doulton nursery-rhyme tile panels that used to decorate the children's ward inside have recently been removed and resited at nearby St Thomas'.

53 THE BEEHIVE PUBLIC HOUSE
227 High St, Brentford, Middlesex
Date: c. 1907
Architects: Nowell, Parr & A E Kates

Although not remarkable in itself, this pub is a good example of the many to be found in London and elsewhere that were faced with coloured Doultonware during the early years of this century. Many have interesting Art Nouveau details, but these have frequently been obscured by later coats of paint.

54 RICHARD EVE MEMORIAL
Brinton Park, New Rd, Kidderminster, Worcs
Date: 1900
Architect: Meredith & Pritchard
Sculptors: J Broad

This is a rare example of a fountain in Doultonware that survives in good condition. The structure is predominantly brown, green and gold, with four inset relief multicolour panels depicting stylised fishes. Set above one of these is a portrait roundel by Broad of Richard Eve, a prominent local Freemason. Meredith and Pritchard designed a number of other similar memorials and fountains in conjunction with Doulton, including the Coronation Fountain, Leyton, Essex, the Queen Victoria Memorial, Malacca, East Indies, and the Victoria Park Fountain, Kingston-on-Thames, Surrey.

55 MEMORIAL TO J HULME
Burslem Cemetery, Burslem, Stoke-on-Trent
Date: 1905
Sculptor: J Broad

Although a number of funerary monuments were constructed in Doultonware, few have survived the combined assaults of weather and vandals. Although badly damaged, this example is still impressive. A tall pyramid crowned with an urn surmounts the grave, while to the front a free-standing angel figure in classical style stands holding a type of portable organ. The base is inset with panels illustrating local views and relating the qualities and virtues of Mr Hulme. Other smaller and less significant Doultonware memorials are known to survive, particularly in the cemeteries of South London.

FAIENCE TILING, TILE PANELS AND DECORATIVE INTERIORS

56 HOTEL CECIL, INTERIOR (DESTROYED)
Strand, London WC2

52 DOULTONWARE DETAILS

54 RICHARD EVE MEMORIAL

56 THE SMOKING ROOM

Date: 1896
Architects: Perry & Reed
Designer: W P Rix
Illustration: *The Opulent Eye*,
N Cooper, pl. 76

Among the most impressive public
suites in this large hotel were the
Indian Apartments, decorated
throughout in blue, yellow, green and
brown Doulton faience. The walls of
the dining, smoking and billiard
rooms were lined with hand-painted
tiles, and the pillars were decorated
with relief moulded tiles all in
'Indian' patterns.

57 HOLBORN RESTAURANT (DESTROYED)

High Holborn, London WC1
Date: 1883–5, 1894
Architects: Archer & Green,
T E Colcutt

Doulton were responsible for the
decoration of the Grill Room, one of a
suite of rooms decorated with
coloured faience.

58 QUEEN ALEXANDRA'S HOUSE, INTERIOR

Kensington Gore, London SW7
Date: 1887
Architect: C P Clarke
Tile designer/painters: J Eyre,
J H McLennan, W J Nunn & E Lewis

Sir Henry Doulton donated the extensive ceramic decorations used in this
building, originally a hostel for
students of the arts. The entrance hall
is lined with green faience in an
elaborate Jacobean style, while in the
sitting room there is a faience fireplace in Gothic style. However, the
best feature is the sequence of tile
panels in the dining room; twelve
panels depict famous figures from the
history of ceramics and music, two
show scenes of Western and Eastern
art and two are views of Lambeth.
   By appointment only.

59 FORMER LONDON, EDINBURGH & GLASGOW ASSURANCE BUILDING, ENTRANCE HALL (NOW

57 HOLBORN RESTAURANT

58 TILE PANEL OF DELLA ROBBIA

59 ENTRANCE HALL

DEPARTMENT OF HEALTH AND
SOCIAL SECURITY)
194–8 Euston Rd, London NW1
Date: 1908
Architect: B Pite
Illustration: *Architectural Review*,
1908, Vol. XXIII, pp. 169–76

An unusual scheme of decoration in
Parian ware tinted pale yellow and
sage green. Greek decorative motifs
were used in a very free manner,
resulting in a quite original effect.

60 TILE PANELS, ST LUKE'S CHURCH

Norwood High St, London SE27
Date: 1885
Designers: J F Bentley,
W Christian Symons
Tile painter: J H McLennan

A rare example of panels in the
Vitreous Fresco technique. They were
originally set into blind windows
above the altar, but after recent structural alterations they are now to be
seen in the community centre. They
represent Christ, St George and
various angels.
   Reduced versions of these murals
were shown at the Chicago
Exhibition in 1893.

61 TILE PANELS, ST THOMAS' HOSPITAL

Lambeth Palace Rd, London SE1
Date: 1896
Tile designers: M E Thompson &
W Rowe
Illustrations: *Studio Year Book*, 1906,
p. 228; *Victorian Ceramic Tiles*,
J Barnard, pl. 114

Two children's wards at St Thomas'
were originally decorated with
nursery-rhyme tile panels. The
Seymour Ward has been demolished
but one panel was resited in the new
main reception area. The Lilian Ward
is still intact, but may be demolished
in the near future, in which case the
panels will be removed and resited
elsewhere. On show near the new
children's ward are similar tile panels
recently removed from the Royal
Waterloo Hospital (see 52 above). In

61 TILE PANEL OF SLEEPING BEAUTY,
FROM LILIAN WARD

The Prince awakens
the SLEEPING BEAUTY

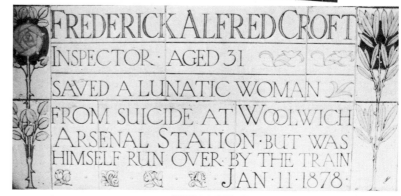

FREDERICK ALFRED CROFT
INSPECTOR · AGED 31
SAVED A LUNATIC WOMAN
FROM SUICIDE AT WOOLWICH
ARSENAL STATION · BUT WAS
HIMSELF RUN OVER · BY THE TRAIN
· JAN · 11 · 1878 ·

62 POSTMAN'S PARK

1904 Doulton produced an illustrated booklet discreetly advertising their nursery-rhyme tile panels and declaring their suitability for hospitals. As a result, many other hospitals were similarly decorated during the early years of this century. The scheme at University College Hospital has now been covered up, except for one panel which was removed and given to the Victoria & Albert Museum and is normally on display at the Bethnal Green Museum. Modernisation has also obscured the Doulton panels at Paddington Green Hospital.

However, more than fifty panels designed by Thompson, Rowe and McLennan are still to be seen in the children's wards at the Royal Victoria Infirmary, Newcastle-upon-Tyne, and others survive at the Buchanan Hospital, Hastings. Nursery-rhyme tile panels were also exported; a scheme still survives in the Wellington Hospital, New Zealand, and some apparently found their way to Poonah.

By appointment only, via Special Trustees Office.

62 MEMORIAL PANELS, POSTMANS' PARK
King Edward St, London EC1
Date: 1871–1917

An unusual series of commemorative plaques set up in this park by George Frederick Watts, the painter, to 'honour heroic self sacrifice'. Each incident is described in stylish script on a large tile and the borders are decorated with either Art Nouveau style flowers and scrolls or a Rennaissance urn pattern. Some panels have motifs which relate directly to the fire or drowning tragedies, for instance a fireman's helmet or a ship.

63 FORMER LYSAGHT'S BUILDING, INTERIOR (NOW RHEEMCO LTD)
Southville Lane, Bristol
Date: 1891
Architect: R M Drake
Illustration: *Builder*, 1897, Vol. LXXII, p. 102

This splendid interior consists of a domed hall with a gallery and staircase entirely lined with cream and gold faience, with intermittant panels in brown and ivory. The relief tiling is decorated with generalised Renaissance details, and the dome has a mosaic frieze depicting shipping through the ages.

By appointment only.

64 KINGS CAFE, INTERIOR (DESTROYED)
Birmingham
Date: c. 1901
Architects: Newton & Cheadle
Designer: W J Neatby
Illustration: *Studio*, 1903, Vol. 29, p. 114

Neatby worked closely with the architects on the design of this café and was wholly responsible for the interior, including the stained glass and metalwork as well as the ceramic murals in Parian ware.

Several other important Neatby schemes have been lost, including the Masonic Hall at the Restaurant Frascati, Oxford St, London, the medallions for the Theatre Royal, Birmingham, and the panels for John Line's showroom, Tottenham Court Rd, London.

65 INTERIOR, WINTER GARDENS (MOSTLY DESTROYED)
Church St, Blackpool
Date: 1896
Architects: Mangnalls & Littlewood
Designer: W J Neatby
Illustrations: *Artist*, 1899, Vol. XXV, pp. 92–3; *British Architect*, 1896, Vol. XLVI, pp. 171–3

This pleasure garden was once extensively decorated with Doulton ceramics but unfortunately most have been covered up or destroyed during repeated renovation schemes. The most striking feature was the entrance arcade, set with 28 tile panels depiction Beardsleyesque ladies representing various jewels and birds.The vaulted roof was lined with relief tiles with varied designs of mermaids, fishes and seaweed, a theme continued

in the ballroom. There was also an elaborate faience staircase.

66 TILE PANELS, FORMER WATNEY RESIDENCE (NOW ST ANDREW'S SCHOOL)
Pangbourne, Berkshire
Date: 1885
Architect: A Waterhouse
Tile designer/painters: J Eyre, J H McLennan, E Lewis

Originally the residence of the Watney family, brewers and Lambeth neighbours of Sir Henry Doulton, this house was decorated with tile panels illustrating various Watney interests. The panels in the dining room include views of the Lambeth embankment, showing the Doulton factory and the Watney Brewery behind it, Lambeth Palace, Derby, the Elephant & Castle crossroads, Boston Harbour in 1735, the Marne, and two panels showing alchemists and pottery merchants.

By appointment only.

67 GENTLEMAN'S LAVATORY
Paisley Cross, Paisley
Date: c. 1900

This public convenience still boasts the original Doulton sanitary fittings and tiling. Relieving the essentially white tiled interior is an inset tile panel depicting Bolton Woods, an incongruously romantic river scene at sunset. Another decorative device is a relief modelled plaque of Paisley's coat of arms.

This interior can be viewed by intrepid ladies, provided that they do not enter alone!

68 TILE PANELS, NEILSLAND HOUSE (DESTROYED)
Hamilton, Strathclyde
Date: c. 1885
Tile designer: W Rowe

This 17th century house, known originally as Highstone Hall, was converted and extended in the late 19th century by a coal magnate. The new billiard room was lined with tile murals painted in an unusually florid style. On one wall were portraits of Scottish writers, including Burns,

63 VIEW OF THE DOME

64 CHIMNEY-PIECE PANEL

65 TILE PANEL FROM THE
ENTRANCE ARCADE

66 ELEPHANT & CASTLE CROSSROADS

68 TILING IN THE BILLIARD ROOM

69 AGRICULTURE & HORTICULTURE

70 DESIGN FOR BENJAMIN FRANKLIN PANEL

Scott and Carlyle, while on the others were views of Loch Katrine and a series of scenes from Scott's novels.

69 TILE PANELS, ST MUNGO VINTNERS (BUILDING DESTROYED)
Queen St, Glasgow
Date: 1893
Tile designer: J H McLennan

The interior of this fine Art Nouveau pub was gutted in 1974. Several fixtures, including two Doulton tile panels were apparently shipped to America at that time. The panels represented Commerce and Industry and Agriculture and Horticulture and were shown at the Chicago Exhibition of 1893.

70 CAFÉ ROYAL, INTERIOR
Register Place, Edinburgh
Dates: 1863, interior remodelled c. 1886
Architect: R Patterson
Tile designer/painters: J Eyre, K Sturgeon, W Nunn & E Lewis
Illustration: *Country Life*, 1969, Aug., p. 1381

The ceramic decorations inside the Café Royal were added several years after the building was erected. Today they survive virtually unaltered. The Oyster Bar is the most spectacular room, richly decorated with coloured relief tiling, and panels painted with putti set into the bar. There are also two tile murals depicting the Cunarder *Umbria* and a Liverpool paddle-steamer.
   In the public bar are six more tile panels showing Victorian inventors. The same designs were shown at the Inventions Exhibition in 1885, and are also believed to have been displayed at the Meadows Exhibition, Edinburgh, in 1886.

71 BOOKING HALL TILING, SINGAPORE TERMINAL STATION
Singapore
Date: 1935
Architects: Swan & MacLaren
Tile designer: W Rowe

This, the largest ever Doulton tile contract, consisted of 7,500 tiles individually painted in matt colours. They formed six panels each over 23 feet high illustrating scenes of land and sea transport and local Malayan industries, including rubber, copra, rice and tin mining.

CARRARAWARE

72a SAVOY HOTEL
Strand, London WC2
Date: 1904 extensions
Architects: T E Collcutt & S Hamp

Doulton's reputation was greatly enhanced by their work at the Savoy. They were responsible for the extensive sanitary arrangements, for the facing of the new extension with Carraraware, and for cladding the earlier buildings in a matching style. This major commission was one of many undertaken by Doulton during the Edwardian period, a period when Carraraware was at the height of its popularity as a cladding material. Some other important examples are listed below:

72b OFFICES
180–1 Fleet St, London, by Flockton & Gibbs, 1901
Illustration: *British Architect*, 1901, Vol. LV, P. 373

72c DEBENHAM'S
Oxford St & Wigmore St London, by Wallace & Gibson, 1907
Illustration: *Architectural Review*, 1908, Vol.XXIII, pp. 362–9

72d DEBENHAM'S HOUSE
Addison Rd, London, by Halsey Ricardo, 1907
Illustration: *Architectural Review*. Vol. XXI, pp. 159, 173

72e OFFICES
12–16 St Vincent Place, Glasgow, By J Miller, c. 1901
Illustration: *Builder*, 1901, Vol. XCII, pp. 543, 787
Doulton Carraraware was also

exported, and was used extensively in Montreal, Toronto and Winnipeg.

73 PAGANI'S RESTAURANT (DESTROYED)
42–8 Great Portland St, London W1
Date: 1896
Architect: C Worley
Sculptor: W J Neatby
Illustration: *British Architect*, 1896, Aug., pp. 128–30

The façade of this restaurant was faced with coloured Carrara, with decorative sculpture by Neatby. Critics at the time admired the building for its varied colour effects and the texture of the material.

74 ASIA HOUSE
31–3 Lime St, London EC3
Date: c. 1885
Sculptor: J Broad

This white Carraraware building has interesting sculptural details, especially the relief panels depicting oriental characters in the Aesthetic style which flank the doorway.

75 FORMER GLOUCESTER HOUSE (NOW OFFICES & THE HARD ROCK CAFÉ)
137 Piccadilly, London W1
Date: c. 1908
Architects: T E Collcutt & S Hamp

Another design by the architects of the Savoy Hotel. It has recently been restored and so its green and white striped Carraraware gable is once again a colourful feature of Hyde Park.

76 EVERARD BUILDING
Broad St, Bristol
Date: 1901
Architects: Essex, Nicol & Goodman
Designer: W J Neatby
Illustrations: *Architect & Building News*, 1971, Sep., pp. 46–7; *Apollo*, 1970, Vol. XCI, pp. 232–4

This well-known façade in brightly-coloured Carraraware has a very unusual decorative treatment. Neatby has created a large-scale ceramic mural, which represents the

72a THE RIVER FRONTAGE

74 ORIENTAL PANEL

history of printing. Gutenberg and William Morris flank the Spirit of Literature, while above in the tympanum is another figure who symbolises the Spirit of Truth and Light.

77 ROYAL ARCADE
Gentleman's Walk, Norwich
Date: 1899
Architect: G J Skipper
Designer: W J Neatby
Illustration: *Artist*, 1899, Vol. XXV, pp. 38, 97–8

The façades of this picturesque arcade are in brightly coloured Carraraware decorated with Art Nouveau motifs. Inside there are friezes of foliage and birds and zodiac symbols in Parian ware.

Other coloured Carraraware arcades include the Emporium Arcade, Northampton, designed in 1901 by Mosley and Scrivener; this vivid white, green and purple structure has been dismantled but the components have been preserved. The elegant, Renaissance-inspired arcade at Chester may also be by Doulton.

78 FORMER TURKEY CAFÉ
(NOW BRUCCIANI'S)
Granby St, Leicester
Date: 1900
Architect: A Wakerley

This whimsical building in the Moorish style was elaborately decorated with coloured Carraraware. The multifoil arched doorway with flanking turkeys has been lost, but some idea of the original design survives in the upper storeys which are crowned by a brightly coloured turkey.

79 FORMER CORONATION BUILDING
(NOW SINGER BUILDING)
76–86 High St, Leicester
Date: 1904
Architect: A Wakerley

Built to commemorate the coronation of Edward VII, this structure was clad in blue-green Carraraware and grey and cream terracotta. This combina-

76 DETAIL OF FACADE   77 DESIGN FOR ZODIAC SYMBOL

77 DRAWING OF EMPORIUM ARCADE

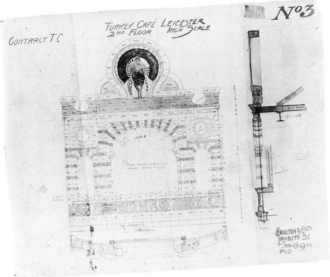

78 DRAWING OF ELEVATION,
SHOWING NUMBERED BLOCKS

81 HAMILTON FOUNTAIN

tion must have originally been quite striking, but is now hidden behind years of dirt. The ground floor has been redeveloped, but some interesting decorative details can still be seen. In each of the façade bays are emblems of the colonies, represented by the various national animals, and the central elevation is decorated with painted tiles depicting naval scenes.

80 BIRD & SONS BUILDING
High St, Deritend, Birmingham
Date: c. 1901
Architect: W T Orton

An unusual combination of red brick and buff Carraraware was used to clad this famous custard maker's works. The building badly needs cleaning but many interesting details can still be seen, including the Dutch style gable with a painted panel of a boat, and the ornamental lettering.

81 HAMILTON FOUNTAIN
Maxwell Park, Glasgow
Date: 1908
Designers: Burnet, Boston & Carruthers

This white Carraraware fountain has suffered badly in recent years. First, it was 'restored' with a thick coat of white oil paint, and now one of the upper basins has collapsed. The fountain was donated to the park by the Misses Hamilton in memory of their brother, Sir William, who was a colonial official of some significance. He is depicted on the central shaft, and a statue of him in hunting attire crowns the top of this splendid structure.

82 PAVILION
Seafront, Torquay, Devon
Date: 1911
Architects: Richards & Garret

This elegant building is faced with white Carraraware with green banded decoration. Its recent cleaning has restored some of the feeling of the Edwardian seaside that these structures epitomise (see also 90 below).
Another seaside pavilion decorated

with Doulton Carraraware was the Kursaal, Ostend, designed by M A Chambon.

83a FORMER SPICERS BUILDING
Newbridge St, London EC4
Date: c. 1935
Architect: F W Troup

The recently restored Spicer Building shows how effectively Carraraware cladding could fulfil modern architects' desires for flat surfaces, shallow mouldings and restrained use of colour. Doulton were very active in this field during the 1920s and 1930s, and among the significant examples are the following:

83b W H SMITH'S BUILDING
Albert Embankment, London, by Ellis, Clarke & Baylis (now demolished)

83c HOUNDSDITCH WAREHOUSE
Houndsditch, London, by Solomon

83d BANNERS BUILDING
Attercliffe Rd, Sheffield, by Chapman & Jenkinson

83e SHEFFIELD & ECCLESHALL CO-OP
Eccleshall Rd, Sheffield, by Johnson

83f ANSELL'S BREWERY
Park Rd, Birmingham, by Stone & Partners

83g HICKMANS & MOULDS PREMISES
Wolverhampton, by Lavender & Twentyman (now demolished)

83h WALTON HOUSE (FORMERLY W H SMITH'S)
Tithebarn St, Liverpool, by Marshall, Tweady & Baylis

These, and many other similar structures, show how well Carraraware could be adapted to fit any style, from Banker's Baroque to International Modern.

83c HOUNDSDITCH WAREHOUSE

83g HICKMANS & MOULD

100

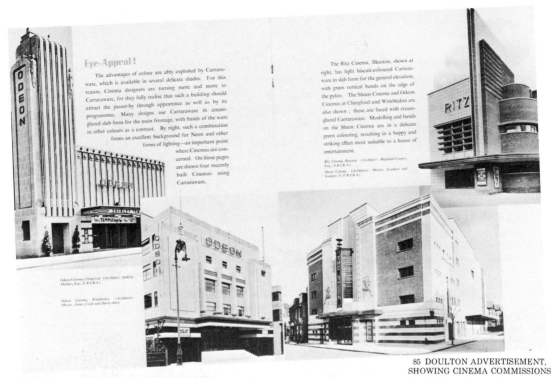

Eye-Appeal!

The advantages of colour are ably exploited by Carrara-ware, which is available in several delicate shades. For this reason, Cinema designers are turning more and more to Carraraware, for they fully realise that such a building should attract the passer-by through appearance as well as by its programmes. Many designs use Carraraware in cream-glazed slab form for the main frontage, with bands of the ware in other colours as a contrast. By night, such a combination forms an excellent background for Neon and other forms of lighting—an important point where Cinemas are concerned. On these pages are shown four recently built Cinemas using Carraraware.

The Ritz Cinema, Ilkeston, shown at right, has light biscuit-coloured Carrara-ware in slab form for the general elevation, with green vertical bands on the edge of the pylon. The Sheen Cinema and Odeon Cinemas at Chingford and Wimbledon are also shown ; these are faced with cream-glazed Carraraware. Modelling and bands on the Sheen Cinema are in a delicate green colouring, resulting in a happy and striking effect most suitable to a house of entertainment.

Ritz Cinema, Ilkeston. (Architect : Reginald Cooper, Esq., A.R.I.B.A.)
Sheen Cinema. (Architects : Messrs. Leathart and Granger, F.F.R.I.B.A.)

Odeon Cinema, Chingford. (Architect : Andrew Mather, Esq., F.R.I.B.A.)

Odeon Cinema, Wimbledon. (Architects : Messrs. Yates, Cook and Darbyshire)

85 DOULTON ADVERTISEMENT, SHOWING CINEMA COMMISSIONS

87 PANEL

84 GREAT WESTERN RAILWAY, ROYAL HOTEL

Praed St, London W2
Date: c. 1935
Architect: P Culverhouse

During the 1930s Doulton Carraraware was used extensively by the GWR during its modernisation programme. The old Royal Hotel was refaced with white Carrara, and many other stations and related buildings received similar treatment, including those at Cardiff and Bristol (Temple Meads).

85 THE SHEEN CINEMA (DESTROYED)

East Sheen, Surrey
Date: 1931
Architects: Leathart & Grainger
Sculptor: E Aumonier
Illustration: *Architect & Building News*, 1931, Vol. CXXV, pp. 2, 6–13

Most cinema designers of the 1930s believed in the virtues of ceramic cladding. It was an ideal background for neon lighting and other forms of publicity, it was durable and easily cleaned. Doulton Carraraware was used on a number of interesting buildings, of which Sheen was the most remarkable. The façade was finished in cream and green with lively modernist green coloured sculpture. Most cinemas of this period have either been demolished or radically altered, but the Ritz, Ilkeston, Derby, by R Cooper, still survives virtually unchanged.

POLYCHROME STONEWARE

---

86 CLOCK, SELFRIDGE'S

Oxford St, London W1
Date: 1931
Architect: A D Millar
Sculptor: G Bayes

This monumental clock over the main entrance represents the Sea of Eternity and shows the Queen of Time standing with wings outstretched on the prow of a ship. Flanking her are sea spirits holding the waxing and waning moons. The group is cast in bronze, overlaid with gold, and inset with Polychrome Stoneware panels. Bayes' original conception was to make the whole group from stoneware, but this was subsequently altered.

87 PANEL, CHILDRENS HOUSE NURSERY SCHOOL

Eagling Rd, London E3
Date: 1925
Architect: C Cowles-Voysey
Sculptor: G Bayes
Illustration: *Architectural Review*, 1926, Vol. LIX, pp. 188–90

This Polychrome Stoneware panel above the doorway shows the Madonna and Child. Bayes was very keen to introduce coloured decoration into architecture, especially in deprived areas. Sceptical colleagues thought this panel would soon be vandalised, but in fact the locals rapidly became attached to it, and cleaned it when it was dirty. Today it still survives amid a sea of desolation and rebuilding.

88 SCULPTURE FOR ST PANCRAS HOUSING ASSOCIATION

88 PANEL OF MERMAID FROM SIDNEY STREET ESTATE

88 BAYES WORKING ON ONE OF THE YORK RISE ESTATE FINIALS

Sidney St Estate, off Chalton St,
London NW1
Date: 1938
Architect: I Hamilton
Sculptor: G Bayes

Hamilton and Bayes worked together
on several St Pancras Housing
Association schemes with the aim of
introducing colourful features into
the environment. Set into the plain
brick walls are several Polychrome
Stoneware lunettes modelled in low
relief with fairy-tale scenes. Subjects
include the Goosegirl, the Little
Mermaid and the Sleeping Beauty. A
novel decorative device was also
introduced into the drying areas;
each washing line post is crowned
with a coloured sculptured finial in
the shape of a boat, a devil, a tailor, an
Xmas tree, etc. Similar features were
included in other St Pancras estates.
At the York Rise Estate, Highgate Rd
& Chetwynd Rd, NW5 the posts are
crowned with dragons, roses and
thistles. However, the duck finials at
the Athlone Estate, Prince of Wales
Rd, have been removed.

89 PANELS AT SOUTH EAST LONDON TECHNICAL COLLEGE
Lewisham Way, London SE4
Date: 1930
Sculptor: G Bayes

This plain brick building is enlivened
by a series of Polychrome Stoneware
panels. Above the entrance are two
large armorial devices, while ranged
round the exterior walls are panels of
animals, birds and foliage in heraldic
style.

90 ROUNDELS AT WHITE ROCK PAVILION
Seafront, Hastings, Sussex
Date: 1927
Architect: C Cowles-Voysey
Sculptor: G Bayes
Illustration: *Builder*, 1922, May,
p. 724; 1927, Dec., p. 1011

This pretty seaside pavilion is
decorated with a series of relief
modelled Polychrome Stoneware
roundels, set effectively against the
white walls. They represent Drama,
Romance, Adventure and Terpsichore
(the muse of dancing). Other
examples of these roundels were

included in one of the St Pancras
Housing Association schemes (see 88
above) and in private garden commissions.

A surviving garden scheme in West
London is decorated with roundels
and also bas-relief panels depicting
classical subjects.

91 RIVER FRONT, HAY'S WHARF
Tooley St, London SE1
Date: 1932
Architect: E Goodhart Rendel
Sculptor: F Dobson
Illustrations: *Builder*, 1932, Feb.,
pp. 348–50; *Studio*, 1932, Vol. CIII,
pp. 152–4

Although the whole building is
memorable, the most impressive
feature is Dobson's striking
sculptural relief. Moulded in gilded
stoneware set into a black granite
background, the sculpture symbolises
the activities of the wharf, dock and
riverside. This modernist sculpture is
unique among Doulton's architectural
work, and is the only known example
of work by Dobson in this material.

90 ROUNDEL

91 DETAIL OF RIVER FRONT

BIBLIOGRAPHY

BOOKS, CATALOGUES AND PERIODICALS RELEVANT TO DOULTON

BLACKER, J F, *The ABC of English Saltglaze Stoneware*, 1922.
DENNIS, R, *Doulton Character Jugs*, 1976.
DOULTON AND CO., *From Sunrise to Sunset*, nd.
DOULTON AND CO., *Pictures in Pottery*, 1904.
DOULTON, H, *Random recollections of a Life*, 1896.
EYLES, D, *Doulton Burslem Wares*, due 1979. *Doulton Lambeth Wares*, 1975. *Good Sir Toby*, 1955. *Royal Doulton 1815–1965*, 1965.
EYLES, D & DENNIS, R, *Royal Doulton Figures*, 1978. *Royal Doulton Character Jugs*, 1979
GOSSE, E, *Sir Henry Doulton*, edited by D Eyles, 1970

CATALOGUES

DENNIS, R, *Doulton Stoneware Pottery*, London, 1971. *Lambeth Art Pottery*, London 1975.
EDWARDS, R, *Lambeth Stoneware: Woolley Collection*, London, 1973.
GOSSE, E, *The Works of George Tinworth*, Fine Art Society, London, 1883.
SHORTER, J, *The John Slater Collection of Doulton Pottery*, Sydney Museum, 1936.
SYDNEY MUSEUM Doulton Exhibition, 1979.

PERIODICALS

ART JOURNAL 1872, p 12, Messrs Doultons Stoneware.
ART JOURNAL 1893, p 110–12 A Ceramic Exhibit for Chicago.
BLACKER, J F, The Burslem Wares, *Connoisseur*, 1912 vol XXXII, p 210 and vol XXXIV, p 136.
ELWOOD, M, The (Doulton) State Dinner Service of Canada, *Bulletin of the National Museum of Man*, Spring 1977.
F. F, Art Pottery at Lambeth, *Leisure Hour*, 1885 p607–16
GODDEN, G, A Tinworth Diary, *Connoisseur*, 1968, Dec, p 230.4. Hannah Barlow, *Apollo*, 1957, Aug, p22–3.
HANDLEY-READ, C, Tinworth's Work for Doulton, *Country Life*, 1960, Sep, p 430–1 and p 560–1.

LLOYD-THOMAS, E, Forgotten Artists of Lambeth Ware, *Country Life*, 1969, Jul, p 227–9.
McCLINTON, K M, Doulton's Art Nouveau and Art Deco Stoneware, *Spinning Wheel*, 1977, Oct, p 23–5.
MILLER, F, Doultons Lambeth Art Potteries, *Art Journal*, 1902, Aug, p .
POTTERY GAZETTE, 1928, Dec, p 1924–9, A Visit to the Doulton Potteries 1933, Apr, p 489–92, Recent Developments at the Royal Doulton Factory.
SPARKES, J, Lambeth Stoneware, *Journal of the Society of Arts*, 1874, May, p 557–70. Further Developments at the Lambeth Pottery, *Journal of the Society of Arts*, 1880, Mar, p 344–57.
STUDIO, 1929, Apr, p 263–8 Modern British Manufacturers. The Royal Doulton Pottery.
VALLANCE, A, The Lambeth Pottery, *Magazine of Art*, 1897, vol XXI, p 221–4.

BOOKS OF GENERAL INTEREST

ASLIN, E, *The Aesthetic Movement*, 1969.
BEMROSE, G M, *19th Century English Pottery and Porcelain*, 1952.
BLACKER, J F, *19th Century English Ceramic Art*, 1911.
GIROUARD, M, *Victorian Pubs*, 1975.
GODDEN, G, *An Illustrated Guide to British Porcelain*, 1974. *An Illustrated Guide to British Pottery*, 1974. *Victorian Porcelain* 1961.
GREEN, R, *Bottle Collecting: a comprehensive price guide*, 1977.
HASLAM, M, *English Art Pottery 1865–1915*, 1975.
HONEY, W, *English Pottery and Porcelain*, 1933.
JEWITT, L, *The Ceramic Art of Great Britain*, 1878 and 1883.
LAMBTON, L, *Temples of Convenience*, 1978.
LLOYD-THOMAS, E, *Victorian Art Pottery*, 1974.
MARTIN, L, *A Collectors Guide to Olde Whisky Jugs*, 1977.
RODGERS, D, *Coronation Souvenirs and Commemoratives*, 1975.
WAKEFIELD, H, *Victorian Pottery*, 1962.

THE AESTHETIC MOVEMENT AND THE CULT OF JAPAN, Fine Art Society, 1972.
VICTORIAN AND EDWARDIAN DECORATIVE ARTS, Handley-Read Collection Royal Academy, 1972.

VICTORIAN AND EDWARDIAN DECORATIVE ARTS, Victoria and Albert Museum, London, 1952.
WILLET COLLECTION OF POTTERY AND PORCELAIN ILLUSTRATING POPULAR BRITISH HISTORY, 1899 now at Brighton Museum.

BOOKS, CATALOGUES AND PERIODICALS OF ARCHITECTURAL RELEVANCE

BALDRY, A L, *Modern Mural Decoration*, 1902.
BARNARD, J, *The Decorative Tradition*, 1973.
Victorian Ceramic Tiles, 1972.
COOPER, N, *The Opulent Eye*, 1976.
CURL, J S, *Victorian Architecture and its practical Aspects*, 1973.
FERIDAY, P, *Victorian Architecture*, 1963.
FURNIVAL, J, *Leadless Decorative Tiles, Faience and Mosaic*, 1904.
GIROUARD, M, *Sweetness and Light*, 1977.
GREATER LONDON COUNCIL *Survey of London* series.
HAMILTON, D, *Architectural Ceramics*, 1978.
HITCHCOCK, H R, *Architecture of the 19th and 20th Centuries*, 1958.
HOBHOUSE, H, *Lost London*, 1971.
LAMBTON, L, *Vanishing Victoriana*, 1976.
MUTHESIUS, S, *The High Victorian Movement in Architecture*, 1972.
PEVSNER, N, *The Buildings of England* series.
RUSKIN, J, *The Seven Lamps of Architecture*, 1849.
SERVICE, A, *Edwardian Architecture*. 1977.

CATALOGUES

JERVIS, S, *High Victorian Design*, Ottawa, 1974.
JOLLEY, D, *George Skipper*, Norwich, 1975.

PERIODICALS

THE ARCHITECT AND BUILDING NEWS.
THE ARCHITECTURAL REVIEW.
THE ARTIST.
THE BRITISH ARCHITECT.
THE BUILDER.
THE BUILDING NEWS.
COUNTRY LIFE.